ARTIFICIAL INTELLIGENCE

COLLECTION

1121 QUESTIONS & ANSWERS

FROM BASIC TO COMPLEX

PART 4

Prof. Marcão – Marcus Vinícius Pinto

1121 Questions and Answers: From the Basic to the Complex - Part 4.

© Copyright 2024- All rights reserved.

The information provided herein is stated to be true and consistent, in which any liability, in terms of inattention or otherwise, for any use or abuse of any policies, processes, or guidelines contained therein is the sole and absolute responsibility of the reader.

Under no circumstances shall any legal liability or fault be held against the authors for any reparation, damage or monetary loss due to the information contained herein, whether directly or indirectly.

The authors own all the copyrights of this work.

Legal issues.

This book is protected by copyright. This is for personal use only. You may not alter, distribute, or sell any portion or content of this book without the consent of the authors or copyright owner. If this is violated, legal action may be initiated.

The information contained herein is offered for informational purposes only and is therefore universal. The presentation of the information is without contract or warranty of any kind.

The trademarks that are used in this book are used for examples or composition of arguments. This use is made without any consent, and the publication of the trademark is without permission or endorsement of the trademark owner and are the property of the owners themselves, not affiliated with this document.

The images that are present here without citation of authorship are images in the public domain or were created by the authors of the book.

Disclaimer:

Please note that the information contained in this document is for educational and entertainment purposes only. Every effort has been made to provide complete, accurate, up-to-date, and reliable information. No warranty of any kind is express or implied.

By reading this text, the reader agrees that under no circumstances are the authors liable for any losses, direct or indirect, incurred as a result of the use of the information contained in this book, including, but not limited to, errors, omissions, or inaccuracies.

ISBN: **9798343136951**

Publishing imprint: Independently published

Summary

1 **THE ROLE OF DATA IN THE AGE OF ARTIFICIAL INTELLIGENCE.** 11

2 **FUNDAMENTALS OF ARTIFICIAL INTELLIGENCE.** 20

3 **GOVERNMENT, POLITICS AND THE FIGHT AGAINST CORRUPTION.** 74

4 **MENTAL HEALTH.** 80

5 **CONCLUSION.** 88

6 **REFERENCES.** 90

7 **DISCOVER THE COMPLETE COLLECTION "ARTIFICIAL INTELLIGENCE AND THE POWER OF DATA" – AN INVITATION TO TRANSFORM YOUR CAREER AND KNOWLEDGE.** 93

7.1 WHY BUY THIS COLLECTION? 93
7.2 TARGET AUDIENCE OF THIS COLLECTION? 94
7.3 MUCH MORE THAN TECHNIQUE – A COMPLETE TRANSFORMATION. 94

8 **THE BOOKS OF THE COLLECTION.** 96

Section	Title	Page
8.1	DATA, INFORMATION AND KNOWLEDGE IN THE ERA OF ARTIFICIAL INTELLIGENCE.	96
8.2	FROM DATA TO GOLD: HOW TO TURN INFORMATION INTO WISDOM IN THE AGE OF AI.	96
8.3	CHALLENGES AND LIMITATIONS OF DATA IN AI.	96
8.4	HISTORICAL DATA IN DATABASES FOR AI: STRUCTURES, PRESERVATION, AND PURGE.	96
8.5	CONTROLLED VOCABULARY FOR DATA DICTIONARY: A COMPLETE GUIDE.	97
8.6	DATA CURATION AND MANAGEMENT FOR THE AGE OF AI.	97
8.7	INFORMATION ARCHITECTURE.	97
8.8	FUNDAMENTALS: THE ESSENTIALS OF MASTERING ARTIFICIAL INTELLIGENCE.	97
8.9	LLMS - LARGE-SCALE LANGUAGE MODELS.	98
8.10	MACHINE LEARNING: FUNDAMENTALS AND ADVANCES.	98
8.11	INSIDE SYNTHETIC MINDS.	98
8.12	THE ISSUE OF COPYRIGHT.	98
8.13	1121 QUESTIONS AND ANSWERS: FROM BASIC TO COMPLEX – PART 1 TO 4.	99
8.14	THE DEFINITIVE GLOSSARY OF ARTIFICIAL INTELLIGENCE.	99
8.15	PROMPT ENGINEERING - VOLUMES 1 TO 6.	100
8.16	GUIDE TO BEING A PROMPT ENGINEER – VOLUMES 1 AND 2.	100
8.17	DATA GOVERNANCE WITH AI – VOLUMES 1 TO 3.	101
8.18	ALGORITHM GOVERNANCE.	101
8.19	FROM IT PROFESSIONAL TO AI EXPERT: THE ULTIMATE GUIDE TO A SUCCESSFUL CAREER TRANSITION.	101
8.20	INTELLIGENT LEADERSHIP WITH AI: TRANSFORM YOUR TEAM AND DRIVE RESULTS.	102
8.21	IMPACTS AND TRANSFORMATIONS: COMPLETE COLLECTION.	102
8.22	BIG DATA WITH AI: COMPLETE COLLECTION.	103
9	**ABOUT THE AUTHOR.**	**104**
10	**HOW TO CONTACT PROF. MARCÃO.**	**106**
10.1	FOR LECTURES, TRAINING AND BUSINESS MENTORING.	106
10.2	PROF. MARCÃO, ON LINKEDIN.	106

Welcome!

As we move into the digital age, Artificial Intelligence (AI) is no longer just a futuristic promise and becomes a palpable reality, permeating almost every aspect of our lives.

This fourth volume of the collection "1121 Questions and Answers: From Basic to Complex" available on Amazon, is another step in the mission to demystify AI and make it accessible to everyone, regardless of their level of familiarity with the technology.

In this volume, we explore a variety of topics essential to understanding the impact of AI on different industries, from theoretical underpinnings to deep, practical questions.

Throughout the pages, you'll find enriching answers about the role of data in government, mental health, and fighting corruption — all critical topics that show how AI can be used to address global and local challenges, while providing opportunities for innovation.

The "1121 Questions and Answers" collection is part of the "Artificial Intelligence: The Power of Data" collection, also for sale on Amazon.

The collection was created with the aim of guiding the reader on a journey through the complexity of AI, offering clear and practical insights into an ever-evolving field.

This book is intended for a wide range of professionals:

- Software engineers, data scientists, and AI developers: They will find tools and insights to expand their skills and face daily challenges.

- Managers and business leaders: they will understand how to implement AI in their organizations, optimizing processes and increasing efficiency.

- Students and academics: they will have a solid foundation in both theoretical foundations and practical applications, essential for their research and projects.

- Politicians and government leaders: will discover how AI can promote transparency, fight corruption, and address complex issues such as mental health and data governance.

The first chapters explore the role of data in the age of artificial intelligence and its fundamentals, highlighting how data is the foundation of AI and allows algorithms to work.

The focus is on processing, analyzing, and curating large volumes of data, with practical examples of its application in sectors such as healthcare and finance, where AI is used to predict disease outbreaks and detect financial fraud.

The second chapter covers the fundamentals of artificial intelligence, explaining essential concepts such as supervised and unsupervised learning, neural networks, and machine learning.

Practical examples include the use of deep neural networks in autonomous vehicles, which learn to make decisions in real time, transforming industries such as automotive.

The third chapter discusses the use of AI in government and in the fight against corruption, showing how technology can increase transparency, detect fraud, and optimize public management.

Data governance and privacy issues are addressed, balancing the advantages and challenges of this advancement.

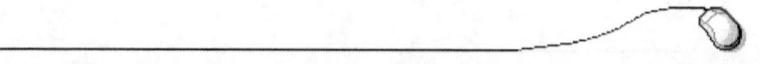

In the chapter on mental health and AI, the focus is on innovations in the treatment of mental disorders, such as the use of chatbots to provide emotional support and algorithms that predict anxiety and depression crises.

Ethical dilemmas related to privacy and human oversight when using AI on such sensitive issues are also discussed.

Completing this volume provides an opportunity to reflect on the impact of AI and humanity's role in shaping its future. AI can solve global problems and improve quality of life, but it also presents ethical and societal challenges that require attention.

The real gain in having the answers to the main questions about AI lies in guiding its development based on values such as fairness, transparency, and responsibility, ensuring that its impact is positive and inclusive for all humanity.

Have good reading and learning!

Prof. Marcão - Marcus Vinícius Pinto

M, Sc. in Information Technology
Specialist in Information Technology.
Consultant, Mentor and Speaker on Artificial Intelligence, Information Architecture and Data Governance.
Founder, CEO, teacher and
pedagogical advisor at MVP Consult.

1121 Questions and Answers: From the Basic to the Complex - Part 4.

1   The role of data in the age of artificial intelligence.

1. How does data drive the development of AI systems?

   Data is the fuel for AI algorithms; with accurate and quality data, AI systems can learn, adapt, and make predictions or decisions with high accuracy.

2. What is the importance of data diversity in AI?

   The diversity in data ensures that the AI system is robust, less biased, and more representative, allowing it to work well in varied scenarios and for a broad demographic of users.

3. How can data limit the effectiveness of AI?

   Low-quality or biased data can lead to incorrect or biased insights, seriously limiting the effectiveness and fairness of AI solutions.

4. How is data privacy managed in AI?

   Data privacy is managed through laws such as GDPR, techniques such as data anonymization, and emerging technologies such as federated computing and differentially private machine learning.

5. What is the relationship between big data and AI?

   Big Data provides the scale of data needed to train complex AI models, making it possible to discover patterns and correlations that are not visible in smaller data sets.

6. How does data analytics empower AI?

Data analytics provides insights that drive the tuning of AI algorithms and the continuous improvement of their predictive models, thereby increasing the accuracy and usefulness of applications.

7. How is data quality evaluated for use in AI?

Data quality is evaluated in terms of accuracy, completeness, consistency, relevance, and timeliness, all of which directly influence the performance of AI models.

8. What techniques are used to protect data in AI?

Techniques such as encryption, data masking, and the implementation of secure architectures are essential for protecting data within AI systems, ensuring that information is used ethically and safely.

9. Does synthetic data have a role in AI?

Synthetic, artificially generated data can help train AI models where real data is scarce or sensitive, allowing for the creation of robust systems while preserving privacy.

10. How does data storage affect AI?

Efficient data storage is crucial for AI because it influences the processing speed and accessibility of data, which are critical to the performance and scalability of AI systems

11. What is the influence of real-time data processing on AI?

Real-time processing allows AI systems to provide instant insights and make agile decisions and is essential in applications such as fraud monitoring and emergency healthcare.

12. What type of data does machine learning depend on?

Machine learning relies on voluminous, varied, true, and fast-paced data (the four Vs of Big Data) to build accurate models and make effective predictions or classifications.

13. Can unstructured data be used in AI?

Yes, AI can work with unstructured data, such as text, images, and sound, using natural language processing techniques and convolutional neural networks to extract information and learn from that data.

14. What are the challenges of integrating AI with Big Data?

Challenges include ensuring data quality and integrity, overcoming storage and processing limitations, and protecting data privacy and security.

15. Can AI help solve the problem of data overload?

AI can automate data filtering and analysis, helping to transform large volumes of raw data into actionable insights, thereby reducing data overload.

16. What is the importance of data visualization in AI?

Visualization helps interpret the results of AI models, allowing users to understand complex relationships of data and insights through intuitive graphical representations.

17. What does it take to train AI models with data?

To train AI models, clean, well-annotated training data, substantial computational power, and specialized knowledge are required to develop and fine-tune learning algorithms.

18. How can AI help with data governance?

AI can optimize data cataloging, anomaly detection, classification, and maintaining data quality, supporting more efficient and regulatory-compliant data management.

19. Is streaming data relevant to AI?

Streaming data, especially in applications that require near-real-time responses, is extremely relevant to AI, such as in recommender systems, social media monitoring, and IoT sensors.

20. How does data interoperability affect the effectiveness of AI?

Interoperability, the ability of disparate systems and organizations to share and utilize the same data, is vital to the effectiveness of AI as it increases the amount of useful data available for modeling and analysis.

21. Data integration plays what role in AI?

Effective integration allows heterogeneous data sources to be combined, enriching the training and performance of AI models and enabling more comprehensive and accurate insights.

22. Can machine learning help with data cleansing?

Yes, machine learning algorithms can identify and correct errors, fill gaps, and standardize formats, improving the quality of data before it is used for model training.

23. Is data curation necessary in AI projects?

Data curation, which includes validating, annotating, and organizing data, is crucial to ensure that input to AI models is of high quality and relevant to the context of the application.

24. How is metadata used in AI?

Metadata provides information about the data, such as origin, date, and format, and is used to organize and locate the data within AI systems, facilitating processing and analysis.

25. Can AI influence data policymaking?

Definitely, AI can provide predictive and descriptive analytics that inform data policymaking, guiding legislation on data privacy, use, and governance.

26. What is the impact of AI on data lifecycle management?

AI can automate and optimize various phases in the data lifecycle, such as collection, storage, use, and disposal, ensuring that data is managed efficiently and responsibly.

27. Does AI demand any specific data standard?

AI benefits from standardized data, which follows a consistent format and is easily accessible, maximizing compatibility between different modeling systems and algorithms.

28. How is data warehousing influenced by AI?

AI can improve data warehousing by guiding the structuring of stored data, enabling complex analysis and advanced reporting, and supporting business decisions based on consolidated, easily accessible historical data.

29. Is anonymized data enough for AI training?

Anonymized data may be sufficient and is often preferred for privacy reasons, especially when AI models focus on patterns and trends rather than individual information.

30. How can AI tools help with data enrichment?

AI tools, through machine learning algorithms and natural language processing, can extract valuable information from datasets, enriching them with new variables and insights for analysis.

31. Can machine learning identify redundant or irrelevant data?

Yes, machine learning algorithms can be used to analyze large data sets and automatically identify and discard redundant or irrelevant information, contributing to the efficiency of data processing.

32. How does AI-powered predictive analytics use data?

Predictive analytics uses historical data and AI algorithms to identify patterns and make projections about future events, aiding in evidence-based and probability-based decision-making.

33. Does data collection for AI require user consent?

Often, yes; particularly in the European Union under the GDPR, data collection for AI often requires informed consent from the user, ensuring compliance and protecting the privacy of individuals.

34. How does data exploration relate to AI?

Data exploration refers to the initial phase of analysis, in which data is probed to identify attributes and potential patterns, directing the development of more effective AI algorithms.

35. Does machine learning need structured data?

While machine learning can work with both structured and unstructured data, structured data is generally easier to manipulate and can lead to faster and more straightforward model training.

36. What tools are common for data management in AI?

Tools such as SQL and NoSQL databases, data processing platforms such as Hadoop and Spark, and programming environments such as Python and R are common for data management and analysis in AI.

37. What is the importance of databases for AI?

Databases are critical to AI because they store the significant amount of data needed to train and operate AI models, as well as enable efficient information retrieval and updating.

38. Can AI help with data harmonization?

AI can be crucial in data harmonization, the process of bringing different data sets into a common standard, using machine learning techniques to transform and consolidate information from multiple sources for integrated analysis.

39. Can machine learning detect anomalies in large data sets?

Yes, machine learning is particularly effective at detecting anomalies, identifying outliers or outliers that may indicate errors, fraud, or rare events within large volumes of data.

40. What is the contribution of AI in big data analytics?

AI contributes significantly to big data analytics by providing automation of data processing and more sophisticated insights, as well as enabling the discovery of hidden trends in complex data sets.

41. Can AI help validate the integrity of the data collected?

Yes, AI algorithms can compare data from different sources, identify discrepancies, and use validation techniques to ensure that the data collected is accurate and reliable before it is used for analysis or training.

42. How does data governance relate to AI?

Data governance establishes the policies and procedures that govern the collection, management, and use of data, and is essential for AI as it ensures that data is used ethically, responsibly, and legally.

43. Can machine learning simplify the integration of complex data?

Machine learning tools are able to recognize patterns in complex data sets, facilitating integration by suggesting automatic mappings and identifying relationships between different data sources.

44. Does AI change the approach to data lifecycle management?

AI adds a layer of intelligence in data lifecycle management by automating data classification, archiving, and even purging according to predefined policies and operational needs.

45. What is the role of data mining in AI?

Data mining is a process of discovering meaningful patterns, and in AI, it is often used to prepare and exploit data to build prediction or classification models.

46. How does AI interact with cloud data platforms?

AI benefits from the scalability and computational power of cloud data platforms to process large datasets and train complex models more efficiently and cost-effectively.

47. Machine learning depends on what type of data infrastructure?

Machine learning requires a robust data infrastructure, which includes high-performance storage, powerful computing capabilities, and efficient management tools to handle data-intensive operations.

48. Can AI influence the way we structure databases?

AI, by informing about the most efficient ways to access and correlate information, can lead to changes in the design of databases, optimizing them for AI queries and advanced data analysis.

49. What is the relationship between clean data and AI?

Clean data refers to data that has been properly corrected, formatted, and enriched; are crucial for AI efficiency as they ensure the accuracy of models and the reliability of results.

50. Can AI generate new data for analysis?

Yes, AI has the ability to generate synthetic data or simulate data that can be used for analysis and to train models where real data may be insufficient or unavailable.

2 Fundamentals of artificial intelligence.

1. What defines artificial intelligence (AI)?

   Artificial intelligence refers to systems or machines that mimic the human cognitive ability to perform tasks and improve themselves based on information collected.

   AI is an area of computer science that seeks to develop algorithms and techniques that allow machines to act intelligently, learn from data, make decisions, solve problems, and perform tasks that would normally require human intelligence.

   AI systems are designed to simulate human mental processes, such as reasoning, learning, perception, language comprehension, and decision-making, enabling computers to perform complex functions autonomously.

   Through machine learning algorithms, artificial neural networks, and other computational approaches, AI is able to analyze large volumes of data, identify patterns, predict outcomes, and optimize processes efficiently.

   An essential aspect of artificial intelligence is the ability to adapt and learn from experience, improving its performance and accuracy over time.

   This is known as machine learning, a subfield of AI that allows systems to automate tasks intelligently and dynamically, without the need for explicit programming for each situation.

2. How does AI differ from traditional software programming?

Unlike traditional programming, which follows explicit instructions, AI can learn from data and experiences, make decisions, and perform tasks in an adaptive manner.

3. What are the main types of machine learning in AI?

Supervised, unsupervised, and reinforcement learning are the main approaches, each suitable for different types of problems and data sets.

4. What skills are required to become an AI expert?

Skills in mathematics (especially statistics), programming, knowledge of machine learning algorithms, and mastery of data processing tools are key.

5. In what segments is AI having a significant impact?

AI is revolutionizing various segments, including healthcare, finance, automotive, information technology, agriculture, and many others.

6. What are the ethical challenges associated with AI?

Ethical challenges include issues of bias, privacy, safety, liability, and the impact on employment, requiring a broad debate on the responsible use of AI.

7. How does AI affect business decision-making?

AI provides data-driven insights that can improve the accuracy, speed, and efficiency of business decision-making, although it should be used with discernment.

8. Are artificial intelligence and robotics the same thing?

No, although often intertwined, AI is a broader field that encompasses the development of intelligent algorithms, while robotics applies these algorithms to physical robots.

9. What is the role of data in machine learning?

Data serves as the foundation for training machine learning models, allowing algorithms to recognize patterns and make predictions or decisions.

10. How can AI contribute to solving environmental problems?

AI can optimize the use of resources, model climate scenarios, monitor biodiversity and pollution, and assist in the creation of sustainable solutions to environmental issues.

11. Can artificial intelligence be creative?

AI has been developed to generate music, art, and literature, simulating creativity to some degree. However, the debate over whether this is true creativity or just advanced imitation continues.

12. What programming languages are common in AI?

Python is the most popular language due to its readability and vast library of AI tools, but others like R, Java, and C++ are also used.

13. Does AI always require large volumes of data?

While many AI models benefit from large datasets, techniques such as transfer learning or reinforcement learning can use less data or learn from interacting with the environment.

14. What is the impact of AI on data privacy?

AI can analyze large volumes of personal data, raising concerns about privacy. Regulations such as the GDPR in Europe were created to protect citizens' privacy in this context.

15. How is AI changing education?

AI provides opportunities for personalization of learning, automated assessment, and access to virtual tutors, fostering innovative teaching and learning opportunities.

16. Can AI eliminate jobs?

Some jobs can be automated by AI, but this can also generate new jobs and require professionals to upgrade their skills to coexist with intelligent machines.

17. What are the limits of AI today?

Today's AI faces limitations such as a lack of deep understanding of the real world, difficulty dealing with atypical situations, and the need for large volumes of training data.

18. How do neural networks work in AI?

Neural networks are inspired by the human brain and are made up of interconnected nodes that work together to identify patterns and make decisions.

19. Can AI revolutionize healthcare?

The application of AI in healthcare promises to improve diagnoses, personalize treatments, optimize hospital management, and accelerate research for new drugs.

20. What is natural language processing (NLP) in AI?

NLP is a subfield of AI that focuses on enabling machines to understand and respond to human language in a natural way, and is used in chatbots, translators, and virtual assistants.

21. How can AI help with cybersecurity?

AI can detect suspicious behavior patterns, predict and respond to cyber threats in real-time, and automate security incident response, improving overall protection.

22. What is the role of ethics in AI research and development?

Ethics guides the responsible development of AI by ensuring that technologies are fair, transparent, and do not cause harm, while protecting the privacy and rights of individuals.

23. Can AI contribute to innovation in traditional sectors?

Yes, AI can increase efficiency, optimize processes, and offer new insights in traditional industries like agriculture, manufacturing, and retail, encouraging innovation and growth.

24. What types of data are most valuable to AI?

Relevant, high-quality, well-annotated data that reflects the context of the problem to be solved is the most valuable for training and developing effective AI applications.

25. What are autonomous AI systems?

Autonomous systems are able to operate independently without human intervention, performing tasks, making decisions, and learning from their experiences and interactions with the environment.

26. How can AI help with disaster management?

AI can analyze data from multiple sources to predict the occurrence of natural disasters, optimize evacuation plans, coordinate emergency responses, and manage resources efficiently.

27. Can AI solve complex problems without human intervention?

While AI can handle many complex problems, human oversight and judgment are still required, particularly in situations that require empathy, creativity, or moral understanding.

28. How does AI influence sustainable development?

AI contributes to sustainable development by helping to monitor natural resources, optimizing energy efficiency, and supporting research into renewable energy and sustainable agricultural practices.

29. Is AI only linked to robots and computers?

No, AI encompasses much more than robotics and computing; It is present in smartphones, cars, home appliances, and many other devices and systems that improve daily life.

30. What advances are expected in AI for the coming years?

Significant advances are expected in natural language understanding, interpretation of emotions, vehicle autonomy, personalized healthcare, and in AI being more accessible and understandable by users.

31. How can AI improve e-commerce?

AI can personalize the shopping experience, optimize logistics and inventory management, create chatbots for customer service, and provide predictive analytics to recommend products.

32. Is AI capable of learning human emotions?

AI can be trained to recognize and interpret human emotions through analysis of facial expressions, tone of voice, and language, but deep understanding of these emotions is still limited.

33. Which industries can benefit the most from AI automation?

Industries such as manufacturing, logistics, finance, and customer service have high potential to benefit from AI-powered automation due to its ability to improve efficiency and reduce costs.

34. How is the safety of AI systems ensured?

The security of AI systems is ensured with secure development practices, regular testing, continuous monitoring, and validation of inputs to protect against manipulation or attack.

35. Can AI help with scientific discoveries?

AI assists in the analysis of large volumes of experimental data, complex modeling of natural phenomena, and the generation of new hypotheses, accelerating the process of scientific discovery.

36. What are the current technical challenges in creating AI?

Challenges include improving the contextual and common understanding of AI, dealing with data and computation limitations, and improving generalization so that AI operates well in various conditions.

37. Can AI predict the future?

AI can make statistical predictions based on past and present data, but it cannot literally predict the future, especially in dynamical systems subject to unexpected changes.

38. How does AI handle uncertain or incomplete data?

AI employs techniques such as fuzzy logic, Bayesian networks, and imputation methods to address uncertainties or gaps in the data, allowing it to make reasonable predictions even with imperfect information.

39. What is the role of AI in precision medicine?

AI plays a key role in precision medicine by analyzing genomes, clinical data, and environmental data to develop personalized treatments and medicines for individuals.

40. How will the evolution of AI affect legislation?

The rise of AI will require new legislation to address issues such as liability, AI rights, and the use and abuse of autonomous systems, ensuring that their implementation benefits society.

41. Can AI face intrinsic biases in data?

AI can perpetuate or even amplify biases if not carefully designed and monitored, requiring active efforts to identify and mitigate biases in training data.

42. What is the importance of benchmarks in AI?

Benchmarks are crucial in AI as they provide benchmarks for evaluating the performance of different algorithms and systems, helping to guide progress in the field.

43. How is deep learning different from traditional machine learning?

Deep learning, an advanced form of machine learning, uses deep neural networks capable of learning high-level data representations, improving pattern recognition capabilities.

44. What are the challenges of interpretability in AI?

Interpretability challenges involve making AI processes and decisions understandable to humans, essential for trust, validation, and regulatory compliance.

45. Can AI help with personalization of education?

AI has the potential to personalize education by adapting content and teaching methods to the needs and learning pace of each student, contributing to a more efficient and engaging educational experience.

46. What is an intelligent agent in AI?

An intelligent agent refers to any system that perceives its environment with sensors, makes autonomous decisions, and acts on that environment to achieve certain goals.

47. How can AI improve public transport?

AI can optimize routes and schedules, predict and manage passenger demand, improve vehicle maintenance, and contribute to more efficient and reliable public transportation systems.

48. Are AI and machine learning interchangeable?

Machine learning is a subfield of AI focused on algorithms that learn from data, while AI is a more umbrella term that includes machine learning, NLP, and other cognitive technologies.

49. What are the scalability challenges in AI?

As AI systems become more complex, the challenge arises to maintain performance by scaling to handle more data, more users, and more varied operating environments.

50. Can AI help in public policies?

AI can analyze large social, economic, and environmental datasets to inform and optimize public policymaking, aiding evidence-based decision-making.

51. How is AI being used in education?

AI in education is applied to personalize learning, automate assessments, facilitate online tutoring, and manage educational systems through predictive analytics to improve student outcomes.

52. How is AI transforming the healthcare industry?

In healthcare, AI contributes to more accurate diagnoses, accelerated drug development, personalized therapies, efficient management of medical records, and surgical robots.

53. What are the applications of AI in agriculture?

AI helps in agriculture with soil analysis, crop monitoring via drone, predicting weather patterns, harvest automation, and optimized management of water resources and inputs.

54. In what area of financial services is AI being employed?

In the financial sector, AI operates in fraud detection, risk management, algorithmic trading, virtual customer assistance, and personalized profile analysis to offer financial products.

55. What is the use of AI in public security?

AI is used in public security for predictive crime analysis, facial recognition in surveillance systems, emergency response management, and social media monitoring for alerts.

56. How does AI influence entertainment and media?

In entertainment and media, AI is used for personalized content recommendation, visual effects creation, market trend analysis, and even in composing music and scripts.

57. What advances does AI provide for autonomous transportation?

AI contributes to autonomous transportation with advanced perception and decision systems, route optimization, traffic sign processing, and predictive vehicle maintenance.

58. How is AI revolutionizing retail?

In retail, AI enables personalized shopping experiences, optimizes inventory management, facilitates demand forecasts, improves logistics, and offers intelligent customer service.

59. How does AI improve the user experience on smart devices?

In smart devices, AI helps understand user preferences, optimize human-computer interaction, offer virtual assistants, and improve the energy efficiency of devices.

60. What is the contribution of AI to the arts and creativity?

AI contributes to the arts and creativity by assisting in the generation of digital artworks, music, literature, and tools that amplify human creative capabilities.

61. How can AI be applied in the gaming industry?

In the gaming industry, AI is used to create intelligent standalone characters, generate dynamic content, improve gameplay, and analyze player behavior to enhance the experience.

62. How does AI act in the optimization of business processes?

AI optimizes business processes through the automation of repetitive tasks, predictive analytics for decision-making, supply chain optimization, and customer service personalization.

63. What are the applications of AI in energy and utilities?

In energy and utilities, AI helps in optimizing energy distribution and consumption, forecasting energy demand, predictive maintenance, and building smart grids.

64. In what ways is AI involved in environmental management?

AI assists in environmental management by facilitating biodiversity monitoring, climate data analysis, modeling environmental impacts, and optimizing the use of natural resources.

65. What is the importance of AI in space exploration?

In space exploration, AI plays a key role in processing data from probes and satellites, autonomous navigation, life systems management, and analyzing images from space.

66. How does AI impact real estate?

In real estate, AI contributes to property valuation, price optimization, generation of virtual views, and improvement in matching buyers with ideal properties.

67. What are the applications of AI in scientific research?

AI accelerates scientific research by automating the analysis of experimental data, simulating complex models, assisting in the formulation of hypotheses, and the discovery of correlations in large volumes of data.

68. How can AI be used to improve customer service?

In customer service, AI is present in chatbots that provide instant assistance, voice recognition systems for natural interactions, and sentiment analysis to better understand customer emotions.

69. How is AI transforming the fashion industry?

AI in the fashion industry drives the creation of computer-generated designs, optimizes supply chain, offers personalized style recommendations, and improves online shopping experience.

70. What is the role of AI in the development of smart cities?

In smart cities, AI helps optimize traffic and resource management, improve public services, increase energy efficiency, and promote sustainability through urban data analysis and management.

71. How does AI contribute to drug development?

AI accelerates drug development by rapidly analyzing compounds, modeling diseases, simulating clinical trials, and identifying candidates for treatments more efficiently and at a lower cost.

72. How can AI help restore the environment?

AI contributes to environmental restoration by monitoring ecosystems, modeling ecological restorations, analyzing satellite imagery to observe changes, and assisting in the conservation of species and habitats.

73. What are the applications of AI in digital marketing?

In digital marketing, AI is used for audience segmentation, campaign personalization, price and inventory optimization, analysis of consumption trends, and measurement of campaign engagement and performance.

74. How does AI improve prediction capabilities in various fields?

AI improves forecasting capabilities by analyzing vast amounts of real-time and historical data to identify patterns and trends, aiding in decision-making in fields such as meteorology, finance, and urban planning.

75. What is the importance of AI in logistics and the supply chain?

In logistics and supply chain, AI is important for forecasting and managing inventory, optimizing delivery routes, demand planning, and for providing real-time visibility and tracking.

76. How can AI help in the fight against climate change?

AI helps in the fight against climate change by improving energy efficiency, analyzing large sets of climate data, contributing to the development of renewable energy sources, and optimizing food production to reduce waste.

77. What are the uses of AI in water resources management?

AI is used in water resources management to monitor and predict water consumption, detect leaks, optimize distribution, improve water quality, and assist in the maintenance of water infrastructure.

78. How is AI influencing product design and engineering?

AI helps product design and engineering by facilitating the simulation and testing of materials, optimizing designs for efficiency and sustainability, and customizing products to meet consumer needs.

79. How can AI help preserve endangered languages?

AI can assist in the preservation of endangered languages through the development of translation and speech recognition technologies, helping to document and teach these languages for future generations.

80. What role does AI play in optimizing energy consumption?

AI plays a key role in optimizing energy consumption by forecasting demand, efficiently integrating renewable sources into electricity grids, and improving the management of smart buildings.

81. How can AI help in the early detection of diseases?

AI contributes to the early detection of diseases by analyzing medical images with high accuracy, identifying patterns in electronic health data, and monitoring vital signs for potential health alerts.

82. How is AI helping oceanographic research?

In oceanographic research, AI assists in the analysis of data collected by underwater sensors, modeling marine ecosystems, predicting ocean phenomena, and exploring inaccessible depths.

83. What are the applications of AI in the food industry?

In the food industry, applied AI optimizes everything from food production, controlling quality, to consumption, with recommendation systems and the development of new products adapted to consumer tastes.

84. How can AI be beneficial for natural disaster management?

AI benefits natural disaster management through data analysis to predict events, optimize evacuation routes, coordinate emergency responses, and assess damage using drones and satellites.

85. How is AI transforming the entertainment industry?

In the entertainment industry, AI is transforming content creation through recommendation algorithms, predictive audience analytics, and automating video and sound editing.

86. What are the benefits of AI in urban traffic management?

AI benefits urban traffic management by analyzing travel patterns, optimizing traffic lights, predicting congestion points, and integrating transportation systems for traffic flow.

87. How does AI influence the future of work?

AI influences the future of work by automating routine tasks, complementing human skills, enabling new forms of remote work, and requiring the development of new skills.

88. How does AI help in the development of sustainable cities?

AI assists in the development of sustainable cities through the optimization of energy systems, waste management, data-driven urban planning, and the promotion of responsible environmental practices.

89. What are the impacts of AI on legal practice?

In legal practice, AI imposes impacts by automating case law research, contract analysis, assisting in predicting trial results, and optimizing legal processes.

90. How can AI be applied in disaster risk management?

AI can be applied in disaster risk management by analyzing large volumes of data to identify areas of risk, modeling disaster scenarios, and creating efficient early warning systems, AI can be applied in disaster risk management by analyzing large volumes of data to identify areas of risk, modeling disaster scenarios, and creating efficient early warning systems.

In addition, AI can be employed in predicting extreme weather events, assessing the vulnerability of communities and infrastructure, optimizing evacuation planning, and coordinating rescue and post-disaster recovery operations.

By utilizing machine learning algorithms and real-time data analysis, AI can provide valuable insights and make quick and accurate decisions to mitigate the impacts of natural disasters and contribute to a more effective and coordinated response in emergency situations.

90. How can AI be applied in disaster risk management?

AI contributes to disaster risk management through large-scale data processing and analysis that allows predicting events, assessing potential risks, and improving response plans.

91. How can AI support environmental sustainability?

AI can support environmental sustainability by assessing the environmental impact of human activities, optimizing the use of natural resources, and developing solutions to problems such as climate change and waste management.

92. What are the applications of AI in wearable and mobile health?

In wearable devices and mobile health, AI analyzes health data collected in real-time, offers preventative insights, helps in monitoring chronic conditions, and promoting healthy lifestyles.

93. How is AI facilitating innovation in the area of renewable energy?

AI is facilitating innovation in renewable energy by optimizing the operation and maintenance of energy devices, forecasting energy production, and integrating renewable sources into the power grid.

94. How does AI contribute to operational efficiency in companies?

AI contributes to operational efficiency by automating processes, improving decision-making with predictive analytics, and optimizing resource allocation and the supply chain.

95. What is the impact of AI on the personalization of streaming services?

AI impacts streaming services by personalizing content recommendations for users, optimizing stream delivery based on bandwidth, and improving the user interface.

96. How can AI help improve climate prediction systems?

AI improves climate prediction systems by processing large sets of weather data, detecting complex patterns, and increasing the accuracy of weather predictions and extreme events.

97. How does AI help the monitoring of patients in the health sector?

AI assists patient tracking through remote monitoring, health data analysis for alerts and preventive insights, and personalized management of treatments and medications.

98. What are the uses of AI in optimizing industrial production?

In industrial manufacturing, AI is used to improve production line efficiency, predict equipment failures, optimize logistics, and personalize product manufacturing.

99. How is AI transforming big data analytics?

AI is transforming Big Data analytics by enabling the rapid extraction of valuable information, uncovering hidden patterns, and providing actionable insights for business and research.

100. How does AI influence older person care technologies?

AI influences age-care technologies by providing monitoring systems, helping to maintain independence with assistive robots, and providing health and emergency alerts.

101. What is good quality data considered for AI training?

Good quality data for AI must be accurate, up-to-date, complete, relevant to the problem, and representative of the reality that the model will attempt to predict or understand.

102. How does the amount of data affect the performance of an AI model?

A larger amount of data often provides more comprehensive training, which can improve the performance of the AI model, as long as the data is of high quality and varied.

103. How can biased data harm AI?

Biased data can lead AI to make biased predictions or decisions, which can cause injustices or errors, especially in critical applications like healthcare and justice.

104. What is data cleansing and why is it important in AI?

Data cleansing involves removing or correcting inaccurate, incomplete, or irrelevant data from the dataset, a crucial step in ensuring that AI operates efficiently and accurately.

105. What types of data are needed to train an AI?

The types of data required to train an AI depend on the application: it can be numerical, categorical, images, audio, text, or time-series data to name a few.

106. How does the data annotation process take place in AI?

Data annotation is the process of labeling or classifying data so that AI can learn from examples. It is done manually by humans or by semi-automated systems.

107. What is the importance of validation and testing datasets in AI?

Validation and testing datasets are crucial for evaluating AI performance and preventing overfitting in training data, ensuring that the model works well on new and unpublished data.

108. How should data privacy be addressed in AI?

Data privacy should be approached in AI with a cautious and proactive approach, considering the impact of artificial intelligence technologies on the collection, storage, processing, and use of users' personal information.

Some key measures to ensure data privacy in AI include:

1. Transparency and explainability. AI systems must be transparent about the data they collect, how it is used, and what decisions are made based on that information. It is essential that algorithms are explainable and auditable, allowing users to understand the reason behind AI-generated recommendations or decisions.

2. Informed consent. Users should be informed about what data is being collected, how it will be used, and have the choice to consent or not to the processing of their personal information.

   Informed consent is critical to ensuring that users have control over their data and can make informed choices about their privacy.

3. Anonymization and data minimization. The personal data collected should be anonymized whenever possible and only the information strictly necessary for the operation of the AI system should be stored.

   Data minimization reduces the risk of sensitive information being exposed and protects users' privacy.

4. Data security. Data security is critical to protecting personal information from unauthorized access, leaks, or privacy breaches.

   Measures such as encryption, authentication, and continuous monitoring must be implemented to ensure the integrity and confidentiality of data in AI.

5. Responsibility and accountability. Organizations that develop and implement AI systems must take responsibility for protecting user data and ensure that ethical privacy practices are followed.

   Accountability mechanisms, such as appointing a data protection officer and conducting privacy impact assessments, are essential to ensure compliance with data protection regulations, such as the General Data Protection Regulation (GDPR).

6. Privacy audits and assessments. Conducting regular audits and privacy impact assessments help identify potential data privacy risks and implement corrective measures to mitigate these issues.

   Continuous review of data collection, storage, and use processes in AI is essential to ensure compliance with privacy regulations.

7. Ethics and data governance. Incorporating ethical principles into the design and implementation of AI systems is crucial for protecting users' privacy.

   Setting clear data governance policies, engaging relevant stakeholders, and adopting ethical standards in AI practice are essential to ensure responsible and ethical use of data.

By addressing data privacy in AI rigorously and responsibly, it is possible to ensure the confidentiality, integrity, and availability of users' personal information, promoting trust and transparency in the use of technology.

Protecting data privacy not only benefits individuals and their personal information, but also strengthens the reputation of companies and organizations that adopt sound privacy practices in the age of artificial intelligence.

109. How has Artificial Intelligence positively impacted education?

Artificial Intelligence has made it possible to personalize teaching, adapting to the individual needs of students. Additionally, it facilitates the assessment and monitoring of students' progress, allowing for more effective interventions.

110. What are the main challenges faced in implementing AI in education?

One of the challenges is the resistance to change and the fear of replacing teachers with technology. Ensuring the privacy and security of student data, as well as the lack of infrastructure and qualification of professionals are also relevant challenges.

111. How can AI contribute to the democratization of access to education?

AI can provide accessible educational resources, allowing students around the world to access high-quality information and learning tools. This can reduce educational disparities and promote inclusion.

112. Why is it important to develop ethical AI systems in education?

Ethics are key to ensuring that AI is used responsibly and does not promote discrimination, bias, or inequality. Developing ethical systems in education is essential to ensure equity and transparency in the educational process.

113. What are the main practical applications of AI in education?

AI can be employed in curriculum personalization, analyzing educational data to identify student achievement patterns, developing intelligent tutoring systems, and creating interactive and adaptive learning environments.

114. How can AI help teachers in their pedagogical practices?

AI can assist teachers in identifying individual student needs, creating personalized educational materials, automated assessment, and efficient classroom management. This allows educators to focus more on personalized teaching and interaction with students.

115. Is it possible for AI to completely replace teachers in education?

While AI has the potential to automate some educational tasks, such as repetitive assessments and personalization of materials, the human presence of teachers is crucial for aspects such as the emotional, social, and ethical development of students, as well as for inspiring, motivating, and encouraging critical thinking.

116. To what extent can AI help in identifying learning gaps?

AI can analyze large educational datasets to identify patterns of student achievement and diagnose learning gaps. With this information, educators can develop more effective strategies to support student progress.

117. What are the benefits of using AI systems to create educational content?

AI systems can generate personalized educational content that is tailored to students' individual needs and learning styles. This increases the relevance of the materials, promotes student engagement, and improves the effectiveness of the teaching-learning process.

118. How can AI help to combat school dropouts?

AI can identify early signs of student disengagement and demotivation, enabling proactive interventions to prevent dropout. In addition, the personalization of teaching provided by AI can increase the relevance and interest of students, reducing the chances of dropping out of school.

119. Why is collaboration between humans and AI systems essential in education?

Collaboration between humans and AI systems in education combines the expertise of teachers with the efficiency and data processing capacity of technology. This synergy can significantly improve the quality of teaching, providing a more personalized and effective approach to student learning.

120. What are the future challenges of using AI in education?

Among the main future challenges is the training of education professionals to effectively integrate AI into their practices, the guarantee of ethics and transparency in the use of educational algorithms, and the continuous adaptation of AI systems to evolutions in the field of education and technology.

119. Why is collaboration between humans and AI systems essential in education?

Collaboration between humans and AI systems in education combines the expertise of teachers with the efficiency and data processing capacity of technology. This synergy can significantly improve the quality of teaching, providing a more personalized and effective approach to student learning.

120. What are the future challenges of using AI in education?

Among the main future challenges is the training of education professionals to effectively integrate AI into their practices, the guarantee of ethics and transparency in the use of educational algorithms, and the continuous adaptation of AI systems to evolutions in the field of education and technology.

121. How can Artificial Intelligence support inclusive education?

AI can make it easier to adapt teaching to meet the needs of students with disabilities by providing personalized resources and assisting in the creation of learning environments that are accessible to all.

122. What are the benefits of AI in student assessment and feedback?

AI can automate and streamline valuation processes, making feedback faster and more accurate. Additionally, it can offer personalized feedback that helps students identify areas of improvement and enhance their performance.

123. How can AI improve the administrative efficiency of educational institutions?

AI can streamline administrative tasks such as enrollment management, schedule organization, and resource allocation, saving educational institutions time and resources.

124. Why is it important to ensure the transparency of AI algorithms used in education?

The transparency of AI algorithms is essential to promote user trust and ensure fairness and impartiality in the educational process. Algorithms must be understandable and auditable to avoid unwanted bias.

125. What are the ethical limits of the use of AI in education?

Ethical boundaries include issues related to student data privacy, the responsible use of technology to avoid manipulation and discrimination, and the need to ensure student autonomy and well-being in a digital environment.

126. What are the challenges of ensuring the security of student data when using AI in education?

The security of student data is a crucial challenge, as the collection and storage of personal information can be targets of security breaches. It is critical to implement robust data protection measures and ensure compliance with privacy regulations.

127. How can AI be used to promote students' autonomous learning?

AI can provide self-assessment tools, personalized study material recommendations, and immediate feedback, allowing students to take greater responsibility for their own learning and progress autonomously.

128. How can AI help in identifying educational trends and needs for improvement in the education system?

AI can analyze large amounts of educational data to identify patterns, learning gaps, and pedagogical trends, providing valuable insights for evidence-based decision-making and continuous improvement of the education system.

129. Why is curriculum adaptation a benefit of AI in education?

Curriculum adaptation benefits from AI because it allows for the personalization of teaching according to the pace and learning style of each student, meeting individual needs and promoting a more efficient and motivating learning environment.

130. What are the educational aspects that can be transformed by the effective implementation of AI?

Aspects such as assessment, personalization of teaching, individualized tutoring, classroom management, development of innovative educational content, and adaptive learning are examples of areas that can be positively transformed by the integration of AI in education.

131. How can AI be used to create more interactive and immersive learning environments?

AI can be used in the creation of simulations, virtual or augmented reality, and adaptive learning platforms that make the educational process more engaging, stimulating and contextualized, favoring knowledge retention by students.

132. What are the impacts of artificial intelligence on teacher training?

AI can assist in teacher training through personalized training platforms, teacher performance evaluation tools, and continuous professional development resources, contributing to improving their pedagogical skills and educational practices.

133. How can artificial intelligence promote the inclusion of students with special needs in education?

AI can offer accessibility features, content adaptation, and individualized support, allowing students with special needs to actively participate in the learning process in an inclusive and diverse environment.

134. Why does AI in education raise questions about educational equity and justice?

The implementation of AI can widen educational disparities if issues such as equitable access to technology, algorithmic biases, and inequality in the quality of education provided are not addressed, which can impact equal learning opportunities for all students.

135. What are the potential risks of over-reliance on AI in education?

Some risks include the loss of human interaction and a sense of community in the classroom, the indiscriminate replacement of teachers with technology, and the possibility of technical failures or algorithmic biases compromising the quality of education offered.

136. How can the use of AI in education impact students' creativity?

AI can stimulate students' creativity by providing new tools and approaches to problem-solving, encouraging experimentation, critical thinking, and collaboration on creative activities and innovative projects.

137. What are the current trends in the use of AI in education?

Current trends include personalization of teaching, adaptive learning, virtual assistants for educational support, predictive analysis of student performance, and intelligent tutoring systems that offer personalized feedback in real time.

138. How can AI contribute to the formation of skills in the twenty-first century?

AI can aid in the development of essential 21st-century skills, such as critical thinking, collaboration, communication, complex problem-solving, and digital skills, by providing opportunities for personalized, hands-on learning in real-world scenarios.

139. Why is it important to employ AI ethically in education?

Ethics in the application of AI in education is essential to ensure integrity, transparency, equity, and respect for the rights of students, teachers, and others involved in the educational process, preventing possible harm and ensuring a safe and inclusive educational environment.

140. What are the future challenges of integrating AI into education?

Future challenges include the need for specialized teacher training in educational technologies, curricular adaptation to include AI skills ensure the cybersecurity of education systems, and address emerging ethical dilemmas related to the use of AI in education.

141. What is the role of Artificial Intelligence in the future of society?

Artificial Intelligence will play an increasingly present and relevant role, impacting various sectors and transforming the way we interact, work, and live.

142. How can AI contribute to significant advances in healthcare?

AI can optimize medical diagnoses, speed up the discovery of new treatments, personalize medicine according to individual patient characteristics, and improve the efficiency of healthcare services.

143. Why is cybersecurity even more crucial with the advancement of AI?

With the increased use of AI, the complexity of cyber threats grows, making it essential to protect sensitive data, prevent attacks, and ensure the integrity of systems.

144. What are the impacts of AI on the labour market in the future?

AI can automate repetitive tasks, boost productivity in various sectors, and create new job opportunities in areas related to technology and the management of intelligent systems.

145. Is it possible to predict the ethical limits of AI in the future?

While it is difficult to predict all of the ethical challenges that will arise with the evolution of AI, it is important to establish clear ethical guidelines and regulations to guide the responsible use of technology.

146. What advances are needed to make AI more accessible and inclusive?

Advances in research, education, talent diversity, inclusion policies, and the development of accessible technologies are key to ensuring that AI benefits all of society.

147. How can AI revolutionise urban mobility in the future?

AI can contribute to improved transportation planning, the development of autonomous vehicles, traffic optimization, and the creation of more efficient and sustainable transportation systems.

148. Why does data privacy become an even more critical concern with the advancement of AI?

Data privacy becomes an even more critical concern with the advancement of AI due to the massive amount of personal information that is collected, processed, and stored, which can result in potential privacy breaches and risks of misuse of the information.

149. What are the ethical challenges of using AI in autonomous decision-making?

Ethical challenges include transparency of AI algorithms, accountability for automated decisions, mitigating algorithmic biases, and ensuring that decisions are fair, impartial, and respectful of individual rights.

150. How can AI be applied to promote environmental sustainability in the future?

AI can be applied to optimize the use of natural resources, predict natural disasters, monitor air and water quality, promote sustainable agricultural practices, and contribute to climate change mitigation.

151. What are the possible applications of AI in education in the future?

In the future, AI can be used to personalize teaching, offer personalized tutoring, analyze student performance data, create interactive and adaptive learning environments, and facilitate automated assessment.

152. How can AI contribute to innovation in sectors such as industry and manufacturing?

AI can be applied to optimize production processes, predict equipment failures, automate repetitive tasks, manage supply chains efficiently, and make industrial operations smarter and more agile.

153. Why will collaboration between humans and AI systems be essential in the future work environment?

Collaboration between humans and AI systems will be essential to combine the creativity, intuition, and interpretive capabilities of humans with efficiency, processing speed, and data analysis of AI, to achieve more robust and innovative results.

154. What are the ethical challenges of the massive deployment of AI in different sectors?

Ethical challenges include the impact of automation on human employment, ethical decision-making by autonomous systems, the security and transparency of AI algorithms, the protection of privacy, and the guarantee of equity in access to technology.

155. How can AI contribute to the creation of smart cities in the future?

AI can be employed to optimize urban services such as transportation, energy, and security, predict citizen demands and needs, improve waste management, and promote sustainability and quality of life in cities.

156. What are the challenges of AI in the area of public security in the future context?

In the future, AI may face challenges in protecting and privacy citizens' data, ensuring fairness and transparency in criminal analysis systems, and the ethics of using surveillance and facial recognition technologies.

157. How can AI be used to boost scientific research and the discovery of new knowledge?

AI can accelerate the analysis of large volumes of data, simulate complex scenarios, identify patterns in scientific data, predict experiment results, and collaborate with scientists to generate new insights and scientific breakthroughs.

158. Why will education and skills development be key to dealing with the evolution of AI in the future?

Education and continuous skills development will be vital to enable people to adapt to the transformations brought about by AI, acquire techno-digital skills, and form a workforce prepared for the challenges of the future.

159. What are the implications of AI in the area of cybersecurity and cyber defence?

AI can be used to identify patterns of malicious activity, prevent cyberattacks, strengthen security systems, and protect networks and critical infrastructure from increasingly sophisticated cyberthreats.

160. Is it possible to predict the impact of AI on the way we relate socially in the future?

The impact of AI on future social interactions could include changes in communication, privacy, trust in information, personalization of online experiences, and the need for ethical regulations to address emerging societal challenges.

161. How could AI influence the global economy in the future?

AI has the potential to drive innovation, increase productivity, create new business models and sectors, transform traditional industries, and impact the labor market, contributing to the global economy in a significant way.

162. What are the concerns regarding autonomy and decision-making by AI systems in the future?

Concerns include the lack of human oversight of critical decisions, the possibility of unpredictable behaviors by AI, liability for harm caused by autonomous decisions, and the need for ethics and accountability in intelligent systems.

163. Why will human creativity and innovation still be essential in a scenario of widespread use of AI in the future?

Human creativity and innovation are unique skills that enable the ability to imagine, create, and solve problems in an original and adaptive way, complementing the capabilities of AI and generating unique and creative solutions.

164. What are the implications of AI in society in terms of inequality and social inclusion in the future?

AI can exacerbate social disparities if policies and strategies are not adopted to promote digital inclusion, reduce technological exclusion, ensure equitable access to education and employment opportunities, and mitigate algorithmic biases.

165. Is it possible to predict the impact of AI on governance and public policy in the future?

AI can influence governance and public policy by providing more accurate data analysis, automating administrative processes, personalizing public services, improving government efficiency, and increasing citizen participation in political decisions.

166. What are the ethical challenges of using AI algorithms in important decision-making processes, such as in judicial systems?

Ethical challenges include the possibility of biases in algorithms, the lack of transparency in automated decisions, accountability for errors and injustices, and the need to ensure fairness and impartiality in the judicial system.

167. How can AI be used to predict and mitigate the impacts of natural disasters?

AI can analyze meteorological, geospatial, and historical data to identify patterns that indicate the possibility of natural disasters, allowing for the adoption of preventive measures, early evacuations, and more efficient responses in crisis situations.

168. Why are privacy and data protection essential concerns in the application of AI in connected devices and systems?

Privacy and data protection are essential concerns due to the large volume of personal information collected and processed by connected devices and systems, and it is essential to ensure the security of information and the consent of users.

169. How can AI be used to personalize customer experience in the retail and e-commerce industry?

AI can analyze customer buying behavior, preferences, and history to recommend personalized products, optimize inventory, improve customer service, and offer a more personalized and satisfying shopping experience.

170. What are the cybersecurity challenges associated with the increasingly frequent use of autonomous systems and smart devices?

Cybersecurity challenges include network vulnerabilities, hacker attacks, theft of sensitive information, data manipulation, and the difficulty of ensuring the integrity and security of interconnected autonomous systems.

171. Is it possible to predict the changes in the workforce and the job market due to AI-driven automation in the near future?

Yes, it is possible to predict some of the changes in the workforce and the job market arising from AI-driven automation in the near future.

The increasing adoption of artificial intelligence and automation technologies is gradually transforming the nature of jobs, requiring new skills and competencies from professionals and impacting labor market dynamics in several ways:

1. Automation of routine tasks. Jobs that involve repetitive and predictable tasks are more susceptible to automation, which can result in reduced demand for labor in these sectors. Many administrative, operational, and production functions can be automated, leading to the reconfiguration of various segments of the workforce.

2. Emergence of new professions and skills. Automation is also driving the creation of new professions and skills in demand in the labor market. Roles related to programming, data analysis, artificial intelligence, cybersecurity, robotics, and other areas of technology are in high demand and tend to grow as organizations seek professionals capable of dealing with new technologies.

3. Emphasis on human skills. With automated tasks being taken over by machines, unique human skills such as creativity, empathy, critical thinking, and soft skills are becoming increasingly valued. Professionals who have the ability to collaborate, solve complex problems, and adapt to change will have a competitive advantage in the job market.

4. Need for recycling and continuous learning. The speed of changes in the labor market due to automation requires workers to be willing and prepared to recycle their skills and knowledge throughout their working lives.

   Continuous learning and constant updating of skills will be essential to keep up with the demands of the ever-evolving job market.

5. Impact on social inequalities. Automation driven by artificial intelligence can also accentuate social and economic disparities, as certain populations may be more vulnerable to the effects of automation.

   It is important to consider strategies to ensure inclusion and equity in accessing employment opportunities in a scenario of increasing automation.

6. Human-machine collaboration. While automation can replace some human tasks, human-machine collaboration can also create new work dynamics.

   Effectively integrating AI technologies with human talent can result in increased efficiency, innovation, and the creation of new job opportunities in emerging industries.

When anticipating the changes in the workforce and job market due to AI-driven automation, it is essential to take a proactive approach to equipping workers with the skills they need to meet the challenges and take advantage of the opportunities presented by this digital transformation.

Resilience, adaptability, and the continuous search for learning and development will be key for professionals who want to stay relevant and successful in an increasingly automated work environment.

172. What are the impacts of AI on the automotive industry and the development of autonomous vehicles?

AI is revolutionizing the automotive industry by enabling the development of autonomous vehicles, improving road safety, optimizing vehicle efficiency, and transforming the mobility experience.

173. How can AI contribute to the prediction and prevention of public health crises, such as epidemics and pandemics?

AI can analyze disease transmission patterns, monitor population health indicators, predict epidemic outbreaks, facilitate contact tracing, and support decision-making by public health authorities.

174. Why are ethics and transparency key in the development and use of AI-based facial recognition systems?

Ethics and transparency are key to ensuring that facial recognition systems are used responsibly, respecting privacy and individual rights, avoiding misuse and discrimination based on physical characteristics.

175. How can AI be applied to climate data analysis and the study of climate change?

AI can process large volumes of climate data, identify patterns, predict extreme events, model future climate change scenarios, and offer insights for the adoption of mitigation and adaptation measures.

176. What are the implications of AI in the area of national security and cyber defense?

AI can be used to detect cyber threats, strengthen the security of critical systems, prevent terrorist attacks, analyze intelligence information, and support military operations more efficiently and strategically.

177. How is AI being applied in scientific research and discovery of new drugs?

AI is being used to speed up the process of discovering new drugs by identifying patterns in large molecular datasets, simulating interactions between chemical compounds, predicting the efficacy of potential drugs, and speeding up the development of more effective and personalized therapies.

178. Why is the interpretability of AI models crucial in sectors such as healthcare and medicine?

The interpretability of AI models is crucial for healthcare professionals and researchers to understand how decisions are made, to be able to trust the systems' recommendations, to detect potential biases, and to ensure the safety and effectiveness of healthcare applications.

179. What are the potential societal benefits of implementing AI systems in areas such as education, health, and public safety?

Potential benefits include access to personalized and quality education, improved medical diagnoses and treatments, crime prevention, and the protection of communities, contributing to a more equal, healthy, and safe society.

180. How can AI be used to optimize the management of natural resources and promote environmental sustainability?

AI can analyze patterns of resource use, predict environmental impacts, optimize production and consumption processes, monitor ecosystems, assist in biodiversity conservation, and support the transition to more sustainable and ecologically conscious practices.

181. What are the main ethical concerns surrounding the use of Artificial Intelligence in autonomous systems, such as self-driving cars and drones?

The main ethical concerns include safety issues, liability in accidents, user privacy, possible damage caused by system failures, and the need to ensure ethical decisions in risky situations.

182. How can Artificial Intelligence be used to improve energy efficiency and sustainability in smart cities?

Artificial Intelligence can be applied to optimize energy use in buildings, manage the electricity grid more efficiently, plan public transport in a sustainable way, and support initiatives to reduce carbon emissions in cities.

183. Why is diversity and inclusion important in the development and implementation of AI systems?

Diversity and inclusion are important to avoid bias in algorithms, ensure representativeness of different communities, promote equity in access to and use of technology, and ensure that systems are developed considering different perspectives.

184. What are the ethical challenges involved in the use of AI for the creation of audiovisual content, such as deepfakes?

Ethical challenges include the spread of misinformation, privacy violations, manipulation of information and images, and the need to develop mechanisms to identify and combat false content created through AI.

185. How can AI be applied to improve water resources management and address challenges related to water scarcity?

AI can be used to predict water demand, optimize the use of water resources, monitor water quality, detect leaks in distribution systems, and contribute to resource preservation.

181. What are the main ethical concerns surrounding the use of Artificial Intelligence in autonomous systems, such as self-driving cars and drones?

The main ethical concerns include safety issues, liability in accidents, user privacy, possible damage caused by system failures, and the need to ensure ethical decisions in risky situations.

182. How can Artificial Intelligence be used to improve energy efficiency and sustainability in smart cities?

Artificial Intelligence can be applied to optimize energy use in buildings, manage the electricity grid more efficiently, plan public transport in a sustainable way, and support initiatives to reduce carbon emissions in cities.

183. Why is diversity and inclusion important in the development and implementation of AI systems?

Diversity and inclusion are important to avoid bias in algorithms, ensure representativeness of different communities, promote equity in access to and use of technology, and ensure that systems are developed considering different perspectives.

184. What are the ethical challenges involved in the use of AI for the creation of audiovisual content, such as deepfakes?

Ethical challenges include the spread of misinformation, privacy violations, manipulation of information and images, and the need to develop mechanisms to identify and combat false content created through AI.

185. What are the ethical challenges associated with the development of autonomous AI systems for military use?

Ethical challenges include issues of accountability in lethal decisions, respect for international humanitarian law, prevention of abuses, and ensuring human oversight over automated military operations.

186. How can Artificial Intelligence be used to personalize customer experience on video streaming platforms?

AI can analyze user preferences, viewing history, and demographics to recommend personalized content, increase engagement, and improve customer satisfaction.

187. Why is the interpretability of AI models essential for areas such as healthcare, where the accuracy of decisions is crucial?

The interpretability of AI models is critical for healthcare professionals to understand the reasoning behind recommendations, verify the reliability of diagnoses, and gain insights into clinical decisions.

188. What are the impacts of AI on the financial industry with regard to fraud detection and financial crime prevention?

AI makes it possible to analyze large volumes of financial data in real-time, identify suspicious patterns, detect fraudulent transactions, and prevent illicit activities in the banking and financial system.

189. How is AI being used to improve efficiency and sustainability in food production in agriculture?

AI allows for crop monitoring, optimization of cultivation processes, harvest forecasting, saving water resources, and reducing the use of pesticides, contributing to more efficient and sustainable agriculture.

190. What are the implications of AI on the development of smart and sustainable cities?

AI can be applied to optimize urban traffic, manage waste, monitor air quality, promote the efficient use of energy and resources, predict and prevent natural disasters, improve public safety, and facilitate the provision of smart and personalized services to citizens.

Implementing artificial intelligence-based solutions in smart cities can provide a number of significant benefits, such as:

1. Operational Efficiency. AI can help cities optimize the management of urban resources and infrastructure, improving operational efficiency in areas such as public transportation, waste collection, street lighting, and water and energy services. This contributes to reducing operating costs, increasing sustainability, and improving the quality of life of citizens.

2. Urban Mobility. AI-based systems can analyze traffic data in real-time, predict mobility patterns, optimize public and private transport routes, and facilitate traffic management, resulting in faster, safer, and more efficient commuting in the city.

3. Environmental Sustainability. AI can be used to monitor air quality, predict pollution levels, identify sources of harmful emissions, and promote sustainable urban development practices.

   By implementing smart solutions to reduce environmental impact, cities can move towards a greener and more responsible development model.

4. Resilience and Security. AI can improve the ability to predict and respond to natural disasters such as floods, fires, and earthquakes, allowing for preventative action and a faster and more effective response in emergency situations.

   Additionally, utilizing AI-based surveillance systems can improve public safety and crime prevention.

5. Improvement of Quality of Life. By integrating AI into urban services, such as health, education, transportation, and social assistance, cities can offer more personalized and efficient solutions to citizens, promoting a better quality of life and well-being for the population.

   The availability of smart and personalized services, such as virtual assistants for public information, AI-based health systems, online education platforms, and sustainable transportation solutions, can facilitate access to resources and improve citizens' experience in everyday life.

6. Innovation and Economic Growth. The implementation of AI technologies in smart cities can boost innovation, attract investment, stimulate economic growth, and generate job opportunities in emerging sectors of the digital economy. Creating innovation ecosystems and fostering technological entrepreneurship can strengthen the competitiveness of cities and boost long-term sustainable development.

191. How is Artificial Intelligence being used in the field of health for the diagnosis and treatment of complex diseases?

AI is used for medical image analysis, identifying patterns in clinical data, developing personalized therapies, predicting diseases based on risk factors, and supporting more accurate and effective clinical decisions.

192. Why are ethics and transparency key issues in the implementation of AI-based facial recognition systems?

Ethics and transparency are key to ensuring the protection of privacy, preventing the misuse of biometric data, avoiding discrimination and mass monitoring, and ensuring that facial recognition is used responsibly and ethically.

193. What are the challenges related to cybersecurity in the era of Artificial Intelligence and the Internet of Things (IoT)?

Challenges include protecting connected devices, preventing cyberattacks, the vulnerability of automated systems, data privacy, and the need for more robust security standards and protocols.

194. How can AI be employed in the development of more sophisticated and personalized virtual assistants for businesses and consumers?

AI enables natural language understanding, more contextual interactions, faster and more accurate responses, personalization of recommendations, and more efficient services, improving the user's experience with virtual assistants.

195. What are the implications of AI in education, with regard to personalizing teaching and identifying individual learners' needs?

AI can analyze student performance, adapt learning content, provide personalized feedback, identify specific difficulties, and promote more adaptive and effective education.

196. How is Artificial Intelligence being used in the field of scientific research, contributing to discoveries and advances in various areas of knowledge?

AI is applied in the analysis of large data sets, identification of complex patterns, simulations of experiments, acceleration of discoveries in medicine, chemistry, physics, biology, and other scientific disciplines.

197. Why is collaboration between humans and Artificial Intelligence systems crucial for the development and improvement of AI technologies?

The collaboration makes it possible to combine human reasoning, creativity and intuition with the computational efficiency and processing capacity of AI, generating more innovative, ethical and socially responsible solutions.

198. What are the ethical and legal challenges related to the use of AI algorithms in recruitment and selection processes?

Challenges include the risk of discriminatory bias in algorithms, candidate privacy, transparency in hiring decisions, the protection of sensitive data, and the need to ensure fairness and diversity in selections.

199. How can Artificial Intelligence be applied to predict and mitigate the impacts of climate change in various regions of the world?

AI is used for climate data analysis, modeling future scenarios, predicting extreme events, identifying vulnerabilities, developing adaptation and mitigation strategies, and supporting sustainable environmental policies.

200. What are the potential benefits of using AI systems in the area of public security and in the fight against crime?

Benefits include analyzing data for crime prevention, identifying crime patterns, optimizing police resources, improving criminal investigation, predicting incidents, and promoting a more proactive and effective approach to fighting crime.

201. How can AI be applied to improve water resources management and address challenges related to water scarcity?

AI can be used to predict water demand, optimize the use of water resources, monitor water quality, detect leaks in distribution systems, and contribute to the preservation of human resources.

201. How is Artificial Intelligence being applied in the area of art and creativity, boosting the production of innovative and collaborative works?

AI is used in music generation, visual art, creative writing, product design, and other artistic expressions, allowing the exploration of new forms of creation and enabling creative partnerships between humans and algorithms.

202. Why are transparency and accountability essential in the development of AI systems, especially in critical contexts such as the automation of industrial processes?

Transparency ensures that decision-making processes are understandable and auditable, while accountability ensures that mechanisms for supervision and correction of failures are implemented, avoiding negative impacts on industrial operations.

203. What are the impacts of Artificial Intelligence in the area of customer service and customer relations?

AI allows for the personalization of service experiences, agility in customer support, automation of repetitive tasks, predictive analysis of consumer preferences, and improvements in interaction on digital platforms.

204. How can Artificial Intelligence be used to improve the management of natural resources and promote environmental sustainability in areas such as biodiversity preservation?

AI can be used to monitor ecosystems, predict environmental impacts, manage protected areas, develop sustainable agricultural practices, and support the conservation of biological diversity.

205. What are the implications of Artificial Intelligence in the area of remote healthcare and telemedicine?

AI facilitates remote diagnosis, patient monitoring, personalization of treatments, optimization of health resources, improvement in access to medical services, and promotion of more efficient and accessible health care.

206. How is Artificial Intelligence being used to improve traffic safety and the efficiency of urban transport?

AI is applied in the analysis of real-time traffic data, the control of smart traffic lights, the prediction of congestion, the management of public transport fleets, and the identification of patterns that can contribute to the reduction of accidents and the improvement of urban mobility.

207. Why is the interpretability of AI algorithms critical to ensuring the reliability and accountability of the decisions made by these systems?

Interpretability allows users to understand how decisions are made, identify potential biases and errors, provide justification for the results obtained, and ensure compliance with ethical and legal standards.

208. What are the impacts of Artificial Intelligence in the area of financial analysis and investments?

AI is used for financial data analysis, market trend forecasting, detecting investment opportunities, portfolio management, automating trading processes, and improving investment strategies.

209. How can Artificial Intelligence be applied to improve waste management and promote the circular economy?

AI is used to optimize waste collection and recycling, monitor irregular disposal points, identify opportunities for reuse of materials, and reduce the environmental impact caused by solid waste.

210. What are the implications of Artificial Intelligence in the area of cybersecurity and the detection of digital threats?

AI is used to identify suspicious behavior patterns, predict cyberattacks, strengthen defense systems, mitigate security vulnerabilities, protect confidential information, and ensure data integrity in digital environments.

211. What are the main ethical and legal challenges surrounding the use of AI algorithms for decision-making in personnel selection processes?

Ethical and legal challenges include algorithmic bias, discrimination, the privacy of candidates, transparency in decisions, the possibility of human review of choices made by AI, and compliance with personal data protection laws.

212. How can Artificial Intelligence contribute to the personalization of more effective medical treatments and therapies?

Artificial Intelligence can analyze large volumes of clinical and genetic data from patients, identify patterns of response to treatments, predict outcomes of medical interventions, assist in the discovery of new therapies, and support physicians in choosing more personalized treatment options.

213. Why is the interpretability of AI models critical in areas such as health and medicine, where decisions must be reliable and justifiable?

The interpretability of AI models is essential for healthcare providers to understand the correlations and patterns identified, verify the reliability of predictions, gain insights into the reasoning behind the recommendation, and be able to act ethically and responsibly.

214. What are the benefits of using AI-based chatbots for companies in the field of customer service?

Benefits include 24-hour availability, quick responses to frequently asked questions, automation of support processes, reduction of labor costs, and improved customer experience with more efficient and personalized interactions.

215. How can Artificial Intelligence be used to optimize supply chains and logistics of companies?

Artificial Intelligence can analyze inventory, demand, and transportation data and predict product shortage or excess events.

216. How is Artificial Intelligence being used in the prevention of financial fraud and in the security of online transactions?

Artificial Intelligence is used to analyze suspicious behavior patterns, monitor transactions in real-time, identify potential fraud, apply additional security measures, and protect sensitive financial information.

217. Why is data privacy an important concern in the development and implementation of Artificial Intelligence systems?

Data privacy is crucial for protecting users' personal and sensitive information, preventing security breaches, ensuring compliance with data protection regulations, and maintaining public trust in the use of AI-powered technologies.

218. What are the impacts of Artificial Intelligence on the automation of industrial processes and on the productive efficiency of companies?

   Artificial Intelligence can optimize the operation of machinery and equipment, predict failures or necessary maintenance, improve product quality, reduce production costs, and increase efficiency and productivity in industries.

219. How can Artificial Intelligence be used to generate insights from large volumes of data (Big Data) and support strategic decision-making in organizations?

   Artificial Intelligence can perform predictive analysis, identify market trends, segment customers, optimize operations, recommend actions, and support management decisions based on accurate data and information.

220. What are the ethical implications of the use of AI algorithms in justice and public security systems?

   Ethical implications include fairness in law enforcement, the possibility of bias in algorithms, citizens' privacy, transparency in judicial decisions, and the need to ensure that AI technologies respect fundamental rights and principles of justice.

221. How is Artificial Intelligence being applied in the development of autonomous vehicles and in the improvement of traffic safety?

   Artificial Intelligence is used to process sensor data, make real-time decisions, predict movements of other vehicles and pedestrians, adapt to different traffic conditions, and contribute to the reduction of road accidents.

222. Why are the transparency and explainability of AI algorithms key to gaining the trust of users and stakeholders?

The transparency and explainability of algorithms allow users to understand how decisions are made, identify potential biases, verify the integrity of processes, and be able to challenge or correct any mistakes.

223. What are the potential applications of Artificial Intelligence in the area of environmental conservation and ecosystem monitoring?

Artificial Intelligence can be used to identify species at risk, map vegetation cover, monitor threatened habitats, prevent illegal deforestation, and sustainably manage natural resources.

224. How can Artificial Intelligence contribute to the personalization of learning experiences and skill development in educational systems?

Artificial Intelligence can tailor educational content to each student's level of knowledge, offer individualized feedback, identify learning gaps, suggest complementary resources, and promote more personalized and effective education.

225. What are the ethical and social challenges associated with the implementation of Artificial Intelligence technologies in areas such as health and well-being?

Challenges include healthcare data privacy, systems security, algorithmic bias, accountability for automated decisions, equity in access to healthcare services, and the need to ensure that AI technologies are used ethically and responsibly.

3 Government, politics and the fight against corruption.

1. How can artificial intelligence be used to fight corruption in the public sector?

   Artificial intelligence can be applied to the detection of suspicious patterns in financial transactions, analysis of bidding data, monitoring of public spending, and identification of fraudulent practices, contributing to the prevention and fight against corruption.

2. What are the benefits of implementing AI systems in public management?

   The implementation of AI systems in public management can help automate bureaucratic processes, optimize resources, improve service delivery, transparency government actions, and data-driven decision-making.

3. How can data analysis through AI algorithms contribute to the identification of corrupt practices in government agencies?

   Data analysis by AI algorithms can identify anomalies, cross-reference information from different sources, detect misappropriation of public funds, track beneficiaries of suspicious contracts, and provide insights for more effective investigations against corruption.

4. What are the ethical challenges involved in the use of AI in political decision-making processes?

   Ethical challenges include issues of algorithmic bias, privacy of citizens' data, transparency in decision criteria, accountability for implementing automatic policies, and ensuring that AI is used for the common good.

5. How can transparency and accountability be strengthened through the application of AI in governments?

Transparency can be strengthened with the disclosure of open data accessible to the population, accountability through justifiable algorithms, the creation of automated monitoring systems, and the promotion of citizen participation in governance

6. What is the importance of system interoperability and data sharing between different government agencies in the implementation of AI solutions?

The interoperability of systems and the sharing of data between government agencies are essential to ensure the integration of information, the exchange of knowledge, the creation of more comprehensive models, and the efficient use of AI tools throughout the government.

7. How can predictive analytics through AI algorithms help prevent corrupt practices before they happen?

Predictive analytics with AI can identify historical patterns of corruption, predict suspicious behavior, flag high-risk situations, anticipate negative events, and enable the adoption of assertive preventive measures in the fight against corruption.

8. What are the impacts of corruption on the implementation of technology projects, including AI systems, in the public sector?

Corruption can generate distortions in the contracting of technology services, influence the choice of suppliers, compromise the quality and safety of the AI systems deployed, in addition to harming the efficiency and transparency of government projects.

9. How can AI deontology guide the responsible and ethical use of technology in government projects?

AI deontology establishes ethical principles and standards that guide the development, implementation, and monitoring of AI systems, ensuring the responsible, transparent, fair, and safe use of technology in government processes.

10. How can the education and training of public servants on topics related to ethics and the use of AI strengthen governance and reduce the risk of illicit practices?

The education and training of public servants in ethics, transparency, data privacy, and AI governance are essential to promote understanding of the impacts of technology, the proper use of digital tools, and the prevention of inappropriate conduct

11. What are the principles of data governance that should be considered when implementing AI projects in government?

The principles of data governance include defining clear responsibilities, establishing information security policies, ensuring data quality, respecting citizens' privacy, and complying with current regulations.

12. How can sentiment analysis through natural language processing help in assessing the population's perception of public policies?

Sentiment analysis with natural language processing allows you to identify trends, opinions, and sentiments expressed by the population on social networks, satisfaction surveys, and other communication channels, providing valuable insights to improve public policies.

13. How can blockchain technology be used to increase transparency and fight corruption in government processes?

Blockchain technology makes it possible to create immutable and transparent records of transactions, contracts, and government actions, ensuring data traceability, information reliability, and the prevention of mismanipulation.

14. What are the legal and regulatory challenges related to the implementation of AI systems in government agencies?

Legal and regulatory challenges include protecting personal data, holding algorithms accountable, ensuring fairness in automated decisions, complying with cybersecurity regulations, and adapting laws to evolving technology.

15. How can the analysis of social networks and the detection of patterns of behavior contribute to identifying possible cases of corruption involving public officials?

Social network analysis allows you to map connections between individuals, identify influencers, track suspicious interactions, and detect patterns of behavior that may indicate corrupt practices involving public officials.

16. What are the benefits of using AI systems for the management of documents and administrative processes in government agencies?

The use of AI systems for the management of documents and administrative processes makes it possible to automate the classification, organization, and search of information, streamlining bureaucratic procedures, reducing errors, and optimizing the workflow in public institutions.

17. How can predictive data analytics assist in the efficient allocation of resources and the prioritization of investments in public policies?

Predictive data analysis makes it possible to identify trends, predict future demands, assess the impacts of different scenarios, and support strategic decisions on the allocation of resources and investments in priority areas for the development and well-being of society.

18. What are the implications of using AI algorithms in candidate selection processes and promotion of public servants?

The use of AI algorithms in selection processes and promotions in the public service raises questions about transparency, algorithmic bias, impartiality, discrimination, and the need for human oversight to ensure fair decisions, based on objective and ethical criteria.

19. How can auditing AI systems ensure compliance with government norms, standards, and policies?

Auditing AI systems involves verifying the correct functioning of algorithms, assessing the quality of the data used, monitoring for any biases, and complying with ethical and legal standards, ensuring the transparency and reliability of government applications.

20. How can artificial intelligence be used to prevent and detect fraud in bidding processes and public contracts?

Artificial intelligence can analyze behavior patterns, cross-reference supplier information, identify discrepancies in bidding processes, point out signs of irregularities, and contribute to the early detection of fraud, preventing losses to the public purse and ensuring fairness and transparency in government contracts.

AI can also monitor ongoing contracts, identifying possible misappropriation of resources and irregularities, providing subsidies for more effective control and inspection actions.

4 Mental health.

1. How can artificial intelligence be used to assist in the early diagnosis of mental disorders such as anxiety and depression?

Artificial intelligence can analyze patient patterns and behaviors in health data, identifying early signs of mental disorders, allowing for preventive and personalized interventions for the treatment and follow-up of individuals.

2. What are the benefits of applying AI in chatbots and virtual assistants for emotional and psychological support?

Through AI-powered chatbots and virtual assistants, people can access immediate, 24/7 emotional support without the stigma associated with seeking psychological help, promoting mental health and well-being.

3. How can AI algorithms be used to identify behavioral patterns indicative of mental disorders in social networks and electronic health data?

AI algorithms can analyze social media posts, internet search logs, and data from electronic devices to identify behavioral patterns characteristic of mental disorders, helping health professionals make more accurate and earlier diagnoses.

4. What are the ethical challenges related to the use of AI in mental health, such as ensuring patient privacy and confidentiality?

Ethical challenges include the protection of sensitive patient data, transparency in decisions made by algorithms, the prevention of discrimination, the need for informed consent, and accountability for the correct interpretation of information provided by AI.

5. How can sentiment analysis through natural language processing be used to detect indicators of emotional distress in written texts?

Sentiment analysis with natural language processing allows you to identify language patterns associated with negative emotions, such as sadness, anxiety, despair, among others, which are indicative of emotional distress in written texts.

By analyzing word choice, tone of voice, and sentence structure, natural language processing algorithms can identify linguistic patterns characteristic of unfavorable emotional states, aiding in the early detection of potential mental health issues and offering appropriate support to individuals.

This enables early interventions, referrals to qualified professionals, and preventive actions to ensure the emotional and psychological well-being of the individuals in question.

6. What are the advances in detecting neural patterns related to mental health conditions through neuroimaging and AI techniques?

Advances in neuroimaging, combined with AI techniques, make it possible to identify specific neural patterns associated with different mental health conditions, such as anxiety disorders, schizophrenia, and depression, enabling more accurate and personalized diagnoses.

7. How can personalizing psychotherapeutic treatments based on AI algorithms improve mental health outcomes?

The personalization of psychotherapeutic treatments with AI algorithms makes it possible to adapt therapeutic approaches to the individual needs of each patient, considering their specific characteristics, preferences, and responses, increasing effectiveness and adherence to treatments.

8. How can the analysis of behavioral and physiological data collected by wearable devices be used to monitor emotional well-being and prevent mental health crises?

Analyzing data collected by wearable devices, such as smartwatches and activity sensors, can provide insights into users' behavior and physiological reactions, allowing them to identify early warning patterns of mental health crises and trigger proactive interventions.

9. What are the technical challenges in creating AI models for the assessment and prognosis of mental disorders, taking into account the complexity and individuality of these conditions?

The technical challenges involve the need for large volumes of diversified and quality data, the interpretation of subjective symptoms, the consideration of individual and contextual variables, the correct interpretation of emotions, and the adaptation of models to different patient profiles.

10. How can telemedicine combined with artificial intelligence expand access to mental health services in remote regions or those lacking specialized resources?

The combination of telemedicine and artificial intelligence makes it possible to conduct remote assessments, provide online therapy, perform patient screening, monitor treatment progress remotely, and offer ongoing support to patients in regions where access to mental health professionals is limited.

This innovative approach makes it possible to expand the reach of mental health services, reduce geographical and temporal barriers, and ensure adequate follow-up for a greater number of people in need.

11. How can artificial intelligence be applied to help diagnose mental disorders, such as depression and anxiety disorder?

Artificial intelligence can analyze patterns of behavior, symptoms, and patient history, comparing this data with information from medical knowledge bases, helping to identify possible mental disorders and contributing to more accurate and earlier diagnoses.

12. What are the benefits of using AI algorithms in assessing suicide risk in patients with mental disorders?

AI algorithms can analyze a variety of data, such as health history, online behavior, and social interactions, to identify patterns indicative of suicide risk, allowing for early and personalized interventions to prevent such cases.

13. How can artificial intelligence contribute to the identification of genetic patterns related to hereditary mental illnesses?

Artificial intelligence can analyze large sets of genetic data and identify correlations between genetic variants and mental disorders, helping to identify genetic patterns associated with inherited mental illness and develop prevention and treatment strategies.

14. What are the ethical challenges in using AI algorithms for mental health diagnosis and treatment?

Ethical challenges involve protecting the privacy of patient data, algorithmic bias, transparency in algorithms' decisions, equity in access to mental health services, and ensuring that algorithms respect ethical and moral values.

15. How can artificial intelligence be used to identify risk factors for mental disorders in different population groups?

Artificial intelligence can analyze demographic, socioeconomic, behavioral, and health data to identify risk patterns for mental disorders in different population groups, allowing for the implementation of preventive measures and targeted interventions.

AI can identify correlations between variables such as age, gender, living conditions, health history, and exposure to stressors, helping to identify groups that are more susceptible to mental disorders.

Based on these data, mental health policies adapted to the specific needs of each group can be developed, promoting a more effective and personalized approach to the prevention and treatment of mental disorders.

16. How can artificial intelligence contribute to the identification of response patterns to different types of therapies in ais?

Artificial intelligence plays a key role in analyzing clinical data, such as genetic information, biomarkers, and scientific study results, to identify efficacy patterns of existing treatments and potential therapeutic targets.

In addition, AI can accelerate the process of discovering new drugs, therapies, and unconventional approaches to treating mental disorders, contributing to significant advances in the field of mental health.

17. How can artificial intelligence help identify symptoms of mental disorders in children and adolescents?

Through the analysis of behavioral data, medical history, social interactions, and academic performance, artificial intelligence can identify early signs of mental disorders in children and adolescents, allowing referral for specialized evaluation and early intervention.

18. What are the limitations and challenges of applying AI algorithms in the diagnosis of mental disorders?

Some limitations include the lack of diverse and representative data, the complexity of the nature of mental disorders, the need for clinical validation of the results obtained, and the importance of human interpretation to complement the analyses performed by AI.

19. How can artificial intelligence contribute to the personalization of treatments for mental disorders, considering the individual characteristics of each patient?

Artificial intelligence can analyze genetic, biological, behavioral, and treatment response data to identify patterns and predict individualized responses to certain therapies, enabling the personalization of treatments and the improvement of clinical outcomes.

20. What is the role of artificial intelligence in monitoring the progress of mental disorder treatment and preventing relapses?

Artificial intelligence can analyze patient data over time, identify patterns of progress or deterioration, predict potential relapses, and trigger alerts for therapeutic interventions or changes in treatment plans, ensuring continuous and effective monitoring of individuals' mental health.

21. How can artificial intelligence be used to detect changes in the behavior pattern of a patient with a mental disorder, aiming to prevent crises or relapses?

By analyzing continuous monitoring data, such as online interactions, physical activity, sleep patterns, and communications with healthcare professionals, artificial intelligence can identify subtle changes in behavior that indicate potential impending crises, allowing for preventative and personalized interventions to prevent relapse.

22. What are the legal and regulatory implications of the use of artificial intelligence in the context of the diagnosis and treatment of mental disorders?

Legal implications include the protection of patient data privacy and security, compliance with health and data protection regulations, accountability for algorithmic decisions, and the need for regulatory vigilance to ensure the quality and ethics of AI applications in mental health.

23. How can AI be used to triage patients in mental health services, optimizing the flow of care and prioritizing more urgent cases?

Artificial intelligence can be used to quickly analyze patient information, such as symptoms, medical histories, and risk profile, in order to classify and prioritize cases, directing resources and attention to those with the greatest need for immediate intervention.

24. What are the challenges of integrating AI systems into clinical mental health settings, considering the interaction with health professionals and the impact on the decision-making process?

Challenges include the need for training and acceptance of healthcare professionals in relation to technology, ensuring effective collaboration between humans and AI systems, correctly interpreting and implementing AI-generated recommendations, and ongoing oversight to ensure the safety and quality of care provided.

25. How can artificial intelligence contribute to the identification of response patterns to different types of therapies in ais?

Artificial intelligence plays a key role in analyzing clinical data, such as genetic information, biomarkers, and scientific study results, to identify efficacy patterns of existing treatments and potential therapeutic targets.

In addition, AI can accelerate the process of discovering new drugs, therapies, and unconventional approaches to treating mental disorders, contributing to significant advances in the field of mental health.

5 Conclusion.

Throughout this fourth volume of the collection "1121 Questions and Answers: From Basic to Complex", we explore the pillars that support the Artificial Intelligence revolution, from technical fundamentals to practical applications in critical areas such as government, mental health, and the fight against corruption.

The book highlighted the "role of data" as the basis of AI, showing how the processing and analysis of large volumes of information enables algorithms to work efficiently.

We discuss how the "fundamentals of AI" such as supervised learning, neural networks, and machine learning are shaping entire industries, from autonomous vehicles to the personalization of services.

Additionally, we address the impact of AI on "government," revealing how this technology can increase transparency and combat fraud, while also exploring its privacy-related ethical challenges.

Another essential aspect addressed was the application of AI in "mental health", where algorithms and chatbots are being used to support the treatment of emotional disorders, anticipate bouts of depression, and provide emotional support.

These advancements, however, raise ethical questions about the use of personal data and the need for human oversight in such a sensitive field.

Each chapter reinforces the central role of AI in modern society, revealing not only its potential to solve complex problems but also the ethical and social dilemmas that come with its implementation.

Technology, when used consciously and responsibly, can improve the quality of life globally. However, its evolution depends on the decisions we make now.

As we conclude this volume, we are invited to reflect on the deeper implications of Artificial Intelligence for the future of humanity.

AI is not an isolated force; it is shaped by the intentions, values, and choices we make. As a society, we must guide its development with "fairness," "transparency," and "accountability," ensuring that its benefits are widely distributed and its risks carefully mitigated.

This book is just one step in an essential journey in the field of artificial intelligence. This volume is part of a larger collection, "Artificial Intelligence: The Power of Data," with 49 volumes that explore, in depth, different aspects of AI and data science.

The other volumes address equally crucial topics, such as the integration of AI systems, predictive analytics, and the use of advanced algorithms for decision-making.

By purchasing and reading the other books in the collection, available on Amazon, you will have a holistic and deep view that will allow you not only to optimize data governance, but also to enhance the impact of artificial intelligence on your operations.

6 References.

ABBOTT, R. (2016). I Think, Therefore I Invent. Creative Computers and the Future of Patent Law. Boston College Law Review.

ALPAYDIN, E. (2020). Introduction to Machine Learning (4th ed.). MIT Press.

BENDER, E.M., GEBRU, T., MCMILLAN-MAJOR, A., & MITCHELL, M. (2021). On the Dangers of Stochastic Parrots: Can Language Models Be Too Big? In Proceedings of the 2021 ACM Conference on Fairness, Accountability, and Transparency (pp. 610-623). ACM.

BENGIO, Y., DUCHARME, R., VINCENT, P., & JAUVIN, C. (2003). A Neural Probabilistic Language Model. Journal of Machine Learning Research, 3, 1137-1155.

CHEN, J., SONG, L., WANG, X., & RUDIN, C. (2018). Learning How to Exclude: Mitigating Bias in Collaborative Filtering Models. Proceedings of the 24th ACM SIGKDD International Conference on Knowledge Discovery & Data Mining, 1895-1904.

COHEN, J.E. (2012). Configuring the Networked Self. Law, Code, and the Play of Everyday Practice. Yale University Press.

CRAWFORD, K. Ethics and Transparency in Artificial Intelligence. Research in AI Ethics, 2021.

GLIWA, B., MOCHOL, I., BIESEK, M., & WAWER, A. (2019). Samsum corpus. A human-annotated dialogue dataset for abstractive summarization. arXiv preprint arXiv.1911.12237.

GOERTZEL, B. (2014). Artificial general intelligence. concept, state of the art, and future prospects. Journal of Artificial General Intelligence, 5(1), 1.

GOODFELLOW, I., BENGIO, Y., & COURVILLE, A. (2016). Deep Learning (Adaptive Computation and Machine Learning series). MIT press.

GUO, B., Zhang, X., WANG, Z., Jiang, M., NIE, J., DING, Y., YUE, J., & Wu, Y. (2023). How close is ChatGPT to human experts? Comparison corpus, evaluation, and detection. ar Xiv preprint arXiv.2301.07597.

HINTON, G.E., OSINDERO, S., & TEH, Y.W. (2006). A Fast-Learning Algorithm for Deep Belief Nets. Neural Computation, 18(7), 1527-1554.

I., & MITCHELL, T. M. (2015). Machine learning. Trends, perspectives, and prospects. Science, 349(6245), 255-260.

KROLL, J.A., et al. (2017). Accountable algorithms. University of Pennsylvania Law Review, 165(3), 633-705.

KURZWEIL, R. (2012). How to Create a Mind. The Secret of Human Thought Revealed. Gerald Duckworth & Co Ltd.

LECUN, Y., BENGIO, Y., & HINTON, G. (2015). Deep learning. Nature, 521(7553), 436-444.

LEE, A. (2019). The Role of Data Structuring in Machine Learning. Journal of Artificial Intelligence, 20(3), 45-58.

LUNDGREN, J., HALL, P., et al. (2017). Consistent Individualized Feature Attribution for Tree Ensembles. Proceedings of the 35th International Conference on Machine Learning, 3093-3102.

MITTELSTADT, B. D., ALLO, P., & FLORIDI, L. (2016). The ethics of algorithms. Mapping the debate. In Data & Society Initiative. Oxford. Oxford Internet Institute.

MURPHY, K. P. (2012). Machine learning. a probabilistic perspective. MIT press.

MURPHY, R. R. (2019). Introduction to AI Robotics (2nd ed.). MIT Press.

NISSENBAUM, H. (2010). Privacy in Context. Technology, Policy, and the Integrity of Social Life. Stanford University Press.

NOBLE, S.U. (2018). Algorithms of Oppression. How Search Engines Reinforce Racism. New York University Press.

O'NEIL, Cathy & SCHUTT, Rachel. (2013). Doing Data Science. Sevastopol, CA. O'Reilly Media.

RADFORD, A., NARASIMHAN, K., SALIMANS, T., & SUTSKEVER, I. (2018). Improving Language Understanding by Generative Pretraining. OpenAI.

REDMAN, T.C. & SOARES, D. D. (2021). Application of AI in Data Governance. AI Magazine, 37(4), 78-85.

RUSSELL, S., & NORVIG, P. (2016). Artificial Intelligence. A Modern Approach (3rd ed.). Pearson Education.

SHALEV-SHWARTZ, S., & BEN-DAVID, S. (2014). Understanding Machine Learning. From Theory to Algorithms. Cambridge University Press.

SHMUELI, G., & KOPPIUS, O.R. (2011). Predictive Analytics in Information Systems Research. Management Information Systems Quarterly, 35(3), 553-572.

YAMADA, I., ASAI, A., SHINDO, H., TAKEDA, H., & MATSUMOTO, Y. (2020). LUKE: Deep Contextualized Entity Representations with Entity-aware Self-attention. In Proceedings of the 2020 Conference on Empirical Methods in Natural Language Processing (EMNLP).

YAO, L., PENG, N., WEISCHEDL, R., KNIGHT, K., ZHAO, D., YAN, R. (2019) Plan-and-write. Towards better automatic storytelling. In fashion. Proceedings of the AAAI Conference on Artificial Intelligence, volume 33, pages 7378-7385.

ZHANG, Z., CUI, P., & ZHU, W. (2020). Deep Learning on Graphs: A Survey. IEEE Transactions on Knowledge and Data Engineering, 32(1), 15-32.

7 Discover the Complete Collection "Artificial Intelligence and the Power of Data" – An Invitation to Transform Your Career and Knowledge.

The "Artificial Intelligence and the Power of Data" Collection was created for those who want not only to understand Artificial Intelligence (AI), but also to apply it strategically and practically.

In a series of carefully crafted volumes, I unravel complex concepts in a clear and accessible manner, ensuring the reader has a thorough understanding of AI and its impact on modern societies.

No matter what level of familiarity with the topic is, this collection turns the difficult into didactic, the theoretical into the applicable, and the technical into something powerful for your career.

7.1 Why buy this collection?

We are living through an unprecedented technological revolution, where AI is the driving force in areas such as medicine, finance, education, government, and entertainment.

The collection "Artificial Intelligence and the Power of Data" dives deep into all these sectors, with practical examples and reflections that go far beyond traditional concepts.

You'll find both the technical expertise and the ethical and social implications of AI encouraging you to see this technology not just as a tool, but as a true agent of transformation.

Each volume is a fundamental piece of this innovative puzzle: from machine learning to data governance and from ethics to practical application.

With the guidance of an experienced author who combines academic research with years of hands-on practice, this collection is more than a set of books – it's an indispensable guide for anyone looking to navigate and excel in this burgeoning field.

7.2   Target Audience of this Collection?

This collection is for everyone who wants to play a prominent role in the age of AI:

- ✓ Tech Professionals: Receive deep technical insights to expand their skills.

- ✓ Students and the Curious: have access to clear explanations that facilitate the understanding of the complex universe of AI.

- ✓ Managers, business leaders, and policymakers will also benefit from the strategic vision on AI, which is essential for making well-informed decisions.

- ✓ Professionals in Career Transition: Professionals in career transition or interested in specializing in AI will find here complete material to build their learning trajectory.

7.3   Much More Than Technique – A Complete Transformation.

This collection is not just a series of technical books; It is a tool for intellectual and professional growth.

With it, you go far beyond theory: each volume invites you to a deep reflection on the future of humanity in a world where machines and algorithms are increasingly present.

This is your invitation to master the knowledge that will define the future and become part of the transformation that Artificial Intelligence brings to the world.

Be a leader in your industry, master the skills the market demands, and prepare for the future with the "Artificial Intelligence and the Power of Data" collection.

This is not just a purchase; It is a decisive investment in your learning and professional development journey.

Prof. Marcão - Marcus Vinícius Pinto

M.Sc. in Information Technology.
Specialist in Artificial Intelligence, Data Governance and Information Architecture.

8 The Books of the Collection.

8.1 Data, Information and Knowledge in the era of Artificial Intelligence.

This book essentially explores the theoretical and practical foundations of Artificial Intelligence, from data collection to its transformation into intelligence. It focuses primarily on machine learning, AI training, and neural networks.

8.2 From Data to Gold: How to Turn Information into Wisdom in the Age of AI.

This book offers critical analysis on the evolution of Artificial Intelligence, from raw data to the creation of artificial wisdom, integrating neural networks, deep learning, and knowledge modeling.

It presents practical examples in health, finance, and education, and addresses ethical and technical challenges.

8.3 Challenges and Limitations of Data in AI.

The book offers an in-depth analysis of the role of data in the development of AI exploring topics such as quality, bias, privacy, security, and scalability with practical case studies in healthcare, finance, and public safety.

8.4 Historical Data in Databases for AI: Structures, Preservation, and Purge.

This book investigates how historical data management is essential to the success of AI projects. It addresses the relevance of ISO standards to ensure quality and safety, in addition to analyzing trends and innovations in data processing.

8.5   Controlled Vocabulary for Data Dictionary: A Complete Guide.

This comprehensive guide explores the advantages and challenges of implementing controlled vocabularies in the context of AI and information science. With a detailed approach, it covers everything from the naming of data elements to the interactions between semantics and cognition.

8.6   Data Curation and Management for the Age of AI.

This book presents advanced strategies for transforming raw data into valuable insights, with a focus on meticulous curation and efficient data management. In addition to technical solutions, it addresses ethical and legal issues, empowering the reader to face the complex challenges of information.

8.7   Information Architecture.

The book addresses data management in the digital age, combining theory and practice to create efficient and scalable AI systems, with insights into modeling and ethical and legal challenges.

8.8   Fundamentals: The Essentials of Mastering Artificial Intelligence.

An essential work for anyone who wants to master the key concepts of AI, with an accessible approach and practical examples. The book explores innovations such as Machine Learning and Natural Language Processing, as well as ethical and legal challenges, and offers a clear view of the impact of AI on various industries.

8.9   LLMS - Large-Scale Language Models.

This essential guide helps you understand the revolution of Large-Scale Language Models (LLMs) in AI.

The book explores the evolution of GPTs and the latest innovations in human-computer interaction, offering practical insights into their impact on industries such as healthcare, education, and finance.

8.10   Machine Learning: Fundamentals and Advances.

This book offers a comprehensive overview of supervised and unsupervised algorithms, deep neural networks, and federated learning. In addition to addressing issues of ethics and explainability of models.

8.11   Inside Synthetic Minds.

This book reveals how these 'synthetic minds' are redefining creativity, work, and human interactions. This work presents a detailed analysis of the challenges and opportunities provided by these technologies, exploring their profound impact on society.

8.12   The Issue of Copyright.

This book invites the reader to explore the future of creativity in a world where human-machine collaboration is a reality, addressing questions about authorship, originality, and intellectual property in the age of generative AIs.

8.13 1121 Questions and Answers: From Basic to Complex – Part 1 to 4.

Organized into four volumes, these questions serve as essential practical guides to mastering key AI concepts.

Part 1 addresses information, data, geoprocessing, the evolution of artificial intelligence, its historical milestones and basic concepts.

Part 2 delves into complex concepts such as machine learning, natural language processing, computer vision, robotics, and decision algorithms.

Part 3 addresses issues such as data privacy, work automation, and the impact of large-scale language models (LLMs).

Part 4 explores the central role of data in the age of artificial intelligence, delving into the fundamentals of AI and its applications in areas such as mental health, government, and anti-corruption.

8.14 The Definitive Glossary of Artificial Intelligence.

This glossary presents more than a thousand artificial intelligence concepts clearly explained, covering topics such as Machine Learning, Natural Language Processing, Computer Vision, and AI Ethics.

- Part 1 contemplates concepts starting with the letters A to D.
- Part 2 contemplates concepts initiated by the letters E to M.

- Part 3 contemplates concepts starting with the letters N to Z.

8.15   Prompt Engineering - Volumes 1 to 6.

This collection covers all the fundamentals of prompt engineering, providing a complete foundation for professional development.

With a rich variety of prompts for areas such as leadership, digital marketing, and information technology, it offers practical examples to improve clarity, decision-making, and gain valuable insights.

The volumes cover the following subjects:

- Volume 1: Fundamentals. Structuring Concepts and History of Prompt Engineering.
- Volume 2: Tools and Technologies, State and Context Management, and Ethics and Security.
- Volume 3: Language Models, Tokenization, and Training Methods.
- Volume 4: How to Ask Right Questions.
- Volume 5: Case Studies and Errors.
- Volume 6: The Best Prompts.

8.16   Guide to Being a Prompt Engineer – Volumes 1 and 2.

The collection explores the advanced fundamentals and skills required to be a successful prompt engineer, highlighting the benefits, risks, and the critical role this role plays in the development of artificial intelligence.

Volume 1 covers crafting effective prompts, while Volume 2 is a guide to understanding and applying the fundamentals of Prompt Engineering.

8.17   Data Governance with AI – Volumes 1 to 3.

Find out how to implement effective data governance with this comprehensive collection. Offering practical guidance, this collection covers everything from data architecture and organization to protection and quality assurance, providing a complete view to transform data into strategic assets.

Volume 1 addresses practices and regulations. Volume 2 explores in depth the processes, techniques, and best practices for conducting effective audits on data models. Volume 3 is your definitive guide to deploying data governance with AI.

8.18   Algorithm Governance.

This book looks at the impact of algorithms on society, exploring their foundations and addressing ethical and regulatory issues. It addresses transparency, accountability, and bias, with practical solutions for auditing and monitoring algorithms in sectors such as finance, health, and education.

8.19   From IT Professional to AI Expert: The Ultimate Guide to a Successful Career Transition.

For Information Technology professionals, the transition to AI represents a unique opportunity to enhance skills and contribute to the development of innovative solutions that shape the future.

In this book, we investigate the reasons for making this transition, the essential skills, the best learning path, and the prospects for the future of the IT job market.

8.20 Intelligent Leadership with AI: Transform Your Team and Drive Results.

This book reveals how artificial intelligence can revolutionize team management and maximize organizational performance.

By combining traditional leadership techniques with AI-powered insights, such as predictive analytics-based leadership, you'll learn how to optimize processes, make more strategic decisions, and create more efficient and engaged teams.

8.21 Impacts and Transformations: Complete Collection.

This collection offers a comprehensive and multifaceted analysis of the transformations brought about by Artificial Intelligence in contemporary society.

- Volume 1: Challenges and Solutions in the Detection of Texts Generated by Artificial Intelligence.
- Volume 2: The Age of Filter Bubbles. Artificial Intelligence and the Illusion of Freedom.
- Volume 3: Content Creation with AI - How to Do It?
- Volume 4: The Singularity Is Closer Than You Think.
- Volume 5: Human Stupidity versus Artificial Intelligence.
- Volume 6: The Age of Stupidity! A Cult of Stupidity?
- Volume 7: Autonomy in Motion: The Intelligent Vehicle Revolution.
- Volume 8: Poiesis and Creativity with AI.

- Volume 9: Perfect Duo: AI + Automation.
- Volume 10: Who Holds the Power of Data?

8.22 Big Data with AI: Complete Collection.

The collection covers everything from the technological fundamentals and architecture of Big Data to the administration and glossary of essential technical terms.

The collection also discusses the future of humanity's relationship with the enormous volume of data generated in the databases of training in Big Data structuring.

- Volume 1: Fundamentals.
- Volume 2: Architecture.
- Volume 3: Implementation.
- Volume 4: Administration.
- Volume 5: Essential Themes and Definitions.
- Volume 6: Data Warehouse, Big Data, and AI.

9 About the Author.

I'm Marcus Pinto, better known as Prof. Marcão, a specialist in information technology, information architecture and artificial intelligence.

With more than four decades of dedicated work and research, I have built a solid and recognized trajectory, always focused on making technical knowledge accessible and applicable to all those who seek to understand and stand out in this transformative field.

My experience spans strategic consulting, education and authorship, as well as an extensive performance as an information architecture analyst.

This experience enables me to offer innovative solutions adapted to the constantly evolving needs of the technological market, anticipating trends and creating bridges between technical knowledge and practical impact.

Over the years, I have developed comprehensive and in-depth expertise in data, artificial intelligence, and information governance – areas that have become essential for building robust and secure systems capable of handling the vast volume of data that shapes today's world.

My book collection, available on Amazon, reflects this expertise, addressing topics such as Data Governance, Big Data, and Artificial Intelligence with a clear focus on practical applications and strategic vision.

Author of more than 150 books, I investigate the impact of artificial intelligence in multiple spheres, exploring everything from its technical bases to the ethical issues that become increasingly urgent with the adoption of this technology on a large scale.

In my lectures and mentorships, I share not only the value of AI, but also the challenges and responsibilities that come with its implementation – elements that I consider essential for ethical and conscious adoption.

I believe that technological evolution is an inevitable path. My books are a proposed guide on this path, offering deep and accessible insights for those who want not only to understand, but to master the technologies of the future.

With a focus on education and human development, I invite you to join me on this transformative journey, exploring the possibilities and challenges that this digital age has in store for us.

10 How to Contact Prof. Marcão.

10.1 For lectures, training and business mentoring.

marcao.tecno@gmail.com

10.2 Prof. Marcão, on Linkedin.

https://bit.ly/linkedin_profmarcao

www.ingramcontent.com/pod-product-compliance
Lightning Source LLC
Chambersburg PA
CBHW050320230526
45471CB00005B/2279